☆ ☆ ☆
CAMPAIGN
BOOT
CAMP
☆ ☆ ☆

D0071455

For Leo Perez,
A great leader!
All the best,

Christine Pelosi

All the best,

CAMPAIGN ★ BOOT CAMP

BASIC TRAINING FOR FUTURE LEADERS

CHRISTINE PELOSI

PoliPointPress

Campaign Boot Camp: Basic Training for Future Leaders
Copyright © 2007 by Christine Pelosi
All rights reserved, including the right to reproduction in
whole, in part, or in any form.

Production management: BookMatters
Cover design: Lisa Fyfe

Print date: October 2007
Distributed by Ingram Publisher Services Inc.

Library of Congress Cataloging in Publication Data
Pelosi, Christine.
 Campaign boot camp : basic training for future leaders /
Christine Pelosi.
  p. cm.
 Includes bibliographical references and index.
 ISBN 978-0-9794822-0-5 (alk. paper)
 1. Political campaigns—United States. 2. Political
leadership—United States. 3. Politics, Practical—United
States. I. Title.
 JK2281.P39 2007
 324.70973—dc22   2007037752

Printed in the United States of America

Published by:
PoliPointPress, LLC
P.O. Box 3008
Sausalito, CA 94966-3008
(415) 339-4100
www.p3books.com

To my family

Contents

List of Sideboxes

Introduction

My mom says that my political activism began in the stroller. Every year, right before Halloween, we went door-to-door through our apartment building with election leaflets. Then a few days later we returned for trick-or-treating. To this day, my mom is not entirely sure whether the leaflets we handed out had any bearing on the kind of treats we received. Maybe all that excess chocolate from certain neighbors was a coincidence.

It was unfathomable to us then that she would become Speaker of the House nearly forty years later. But politics isn't about the big leap to power; it's about the thousands of steps you take with your neighbors along the way. Millions of Americans are taking those steps every day, from voting to volunteering to full-time community, military, and political service. Each of these Americans has heeded a personal call to service: a voice of conscience that springs from vision, ideas, and values and urges participation in building stronger communities today and a better future for the next generation.

Campaign Boot Camp emerged from my own call to service as a volunteer and strategist engaged in politics and policy.

Why a Campaign? We have a strong tradition of civic activism in our country. Most Americans feel a call to service.

1

Meeting the challenges we face as a country depends on our participation in our democracy. Performing service, and attracting others to it, requires a campaign—a mechanism to work with people in a disciplined way toward a common goal. A winning political campaign is a fusion of a large social movement and a small-business startup. It takes a long-term dedication to values and a short-term, nuts-and-bolts strategy to earn more than half the votes come Election Day.

Why a Boot Camp? It is essential to identify the inspiration, perspiration, and perseverance that transform dreams into actions. In public service, that means excellence at management, message, money, and mobilization. The boot camp model—short, concentrated lessons that respect your time with questions and tools that hone your skills—is ideal for people who want to get a broad sense of the elements of a campaign in a short time. I have used this model in grassroots trainings in my home state of California and as director of the AFSCME PEOPLE/New House PAC Congressional Candidate Boot Camp (AFSCME is the American Federation of State County and Municipal Employees; a PAC is a Political Action Committee). Our Boot Camp offered leadership seminars, regional round tables, virtual trainings, and conference calls showcasing the best practices and lessons learned in management, message, money, and mobilization for over forty challengers across America.

The Boot Camp's online home, ChallengerNET.com, provided worksheets and training resources, updated polls, news analysis, and my *Trail Mix* blog, a periodic report from the campaign arena—on the ground with candidates, their families, and volunteers. Some congressional challengers did not end up running or winning their primaries, but most were quite competitive, and twelve are now members of Congress.

My *Trail Mix* blog covered these challengers as well as additional candidates whose races emerged after May 2006.

Campaign Boot Camp draws on my years of grassroots activism, the Boot Camp trainings, and my *Trail Mix* blog. As *Trail Mix* author, I profiled challenger candidates: Fighting Dems (military veterans), working moms, law enforcement officers, community business owners, public policy experts, and rising young stars representing all the great traditions of America and the independent aspirations of their constituents. You will meet some of these outstanding challengers in the book.

I've had the opportunity to travel around the country two times: first in 1993, touring baseball parks while awaiting the results of the California bar exam; and then in 2006, while blogging about congressional campaigns for *Trail Mix*. Both tours allowed me a community-based introduction to the American people. On my 1993 tour, I studied the architecture of the ballparks, the lore of the game, and the pride of the communities. I paid special attention to baseball's fundamentals—teamwork, hitting, pitching, and fielding—without which no team can win. On my 2006 *Trail Mix* tour, the stakes were considerably higher, but my approach was similar. I studied the architecture of the campaigns, the lore of political traditions, and the pride of the communities, paying special attention to campaign fundamentals—management, message, money, and mobilization—without which no election can be won.

Campaign Boot Camp is built on these fundamentals as they are practiced by people across the political spectrum. The call to service is intensely personal and idealistic, but the path to service is decidedly nonpartisan. As a prosecutor in San Francisco, I sought advice on how to evaluate and try cases from defense attorneys. As chief of staff on Capitol Hill for Congressman John F. Tierney, Democrat of Massachusetts, one of the first management books I read was a manual prepared by the office of Congressman Dick Armey, Republican of Texas. In that spirit, I wrote *Campaign Boot Camp* with an eye on the collective wisdom in strategy and tactics from Democrats, Republicans, and Independents.

Each election cycle is defined by issues, events, and trends. In 2006, a broad range of issues moved voters, but *nothing* shaped the perceptions of the people I met on the campaign trail more than the events of Hurricane Katrina and the Iraq war.

Our first Boot Camp was scheduled for September 2005; then Hurricane Katrina struck, and instead of looking ahead to November 2006, we, like all Americans, were facing the immediacy of the tragedy. AFSCME, a public service employees union, was dealing with the emergency needs of its people in New Orleans, including its Charity Hospital employees on the rooftops trying to medevac patients to safety, and organizing its members to help with Gulf Coast recovery efforts. Meanwhile, on the war front, the news from Iraq was continually grim, with repeated requests for a better plan for our troops, for body armor, for jammers to disrupt improvised explosive devices, and for veterans' care. Some of that advocacy came from our Fighting Dems—veterans running for Congress—speaking out for their colleagues still on the battlefield and for family members praying for loved ones. Both events revealed the fragile social fabric in our country and the sense that America can be better: that we can have a plan to care for all people displaced by tragedy, regardless of class or race; that we can keep our promises to all who defend us; and that our government can act to heal the breach and be as good as its people. To address these challenges, millions of Americans stepped into the breach: volunteers traveled to the Gulf Coast, and tens of thousands more offered financial help; military families and veterans of all generations urged support for our heroes in uniform; dozens of candidates ran for office with vision, ideas, and optimism. But we need more. And to fully address these challenges, we need to build a culture of service where every American is called to vote, and every American is called to participate.

To build this culture of service, we must capitalize on the trends of the 2006 election cycle: the emerging online social networks populated by people eager to connect with one another, to organize, and to make a difference. Many fresh recruits on the campaign trail were volunteers connected with partisan groups like Young Democrats and College Republicans, but just as significant were the people mobilized by progressive netroots (Internet-based grassroots organizers) networks such as MoveOn and the *Daily Kos* community, by conservative networks such as the Club for Growth, by fiercely independent communities such as the Iraq and Afghanistan Veterans of America (IAVA), and by multipartisan coalitions forming around issues. In 2006 these issues ranged from homeland security and civil liberties to stagnant wages and outsourced jobs to budget deficits to education to health care to prescription drugs to stem cell research to gas prices to global warming to retirement and pension security to immigration to election integrity to net neutrality. American politics is being reinvigorated by these new networks of people willing to come together around a shared mission, stay together through challenges, and work together despite the inevitable clashes of personalities and agendas.

The 2006 elections were historic: Democrats gained control of the House and Senate, and a woman was elected Speaker of the House for the first time ever. This book is not an explanation of how the elections were won by the Democrats (or lost by the Republicans) but rather a guide to techniques and tools from the 2006 congressional elections for you to use to prepare to make your mark on history.

The threshold question for anyone who enters public life is this: do you want to *do* something or do you want to *be* something? *Campaign Boot Camp* is for people who want to do something; basic training for future leaders who hear a call to service and are looking for a roadmap of how to transform dreams into actions through connecting with people and organizing with social networks, nonprofits, and policy initiatives. *Campaign Boot Camp* is a how-to guide that sets forth seven essential steps: Identify Your Call to Service, Know Your Community, Build Your Leadership Teams, Define Your Message, Connect with People, Raise the Money, and Mobilize to Win. Each chapter ends with a Get Real exercise to personalize and integrate these ideas into your own scope of service. Whether you're a young mom leafleting your neighborhood or a veteran politician, *Campaign Boot Camp* will help you serve our country and work to achieve your vision.

ONE

Identify Your Call to Service

There are two kinds of people who enter public life:
those who want to *do* something and those who
want to *be* something.   — *Political proverb*

Our democracy requires a binding commitment between
people, a commitment that begins with the earliest actions in
family, school, worship, and community. It is a commitment
that develops over time and experience, based on a call to
service—the vision, ideas, and values that motivate each
public servant.

Each of us has a personal call to service that motivates and
inspires our actions in family, community, and public life.
Whether your public service involves helping a nonprofit
agency achieve its mission, voting or volunteering in an election, mastering the skills of running for public office, study-
ing political science and civics, or networking with your peers
in a community improvement project, everything you do to
engage in democracy begins with your call to service. Your
call to service is your vision for the future, your ideas and
values, and your commitment to achieving the vision by
working in community with others. Whether your household is grounded in social responsibility or politics or workers' rights or civil rights or military service, your call begins
at home with a family ethic, manifests itself in community

7

work, and provides a touchstone for all you do, inspiring you on the good days and strengthening you on the bad days. America's Founders articulated a national call to service in the Preamble to the United States Constitution.

> We the people of the United States, in order to form a more perfect union, establish justice, insure domestic tranquility, provide for the common defense, promote the general welfare, and secure the blessings of liberty to ourselves and our posterity do ordain and establish this Constitution for the United States of America.

The Founders' call to service echoes through the years as a challenge for each generation of Americans to achieve the vision. Indeed, the first official act for every public officer in America is an oath to protect and defend the Constitution. Your call to service tells you who you are, why you serve the public, and how you will fulfill your vision and that of our Founders as set forth in our Constitution. Your actions derive from that call to service.

In assessing your own participation in our democracy, the first essential question is, what is your personal call to service?

ARTICULATE YOUR VISION FOR THE FUTURE

If you had the power to change the world, what would the future be like? A safer America? A freer people? A stronger community? A better-educated workforce? A healthier society? A fairer economy? A national culture of service? First and foremost, you must identify the touchstone of your service: a vision so compelling to you that you would give of your time, energy, resources, and reputation to achieve the vision and to ask others to give of themselves to do the same. Consider the actions you have taken in your community—with nonprofits, local organizations, and/or political campaigns. What kind of future are you trying to build for future generations?

COMMUNICATE THE IDEAS
THAT WILL ACHIEVE YOUR VISION

Our Constitution was a bold stroke—a fusion of ideas, imagination, and intellect that shaped our Founders' vision of the future.

What are the ideas you propose to achieve your vision of the future? How a safer America builds allies and protects us from adversaries? How free people balance security with freedom of speech, worship, and assembly? How a stronger community treats police officers, victims, and criminals? How a better-educated workforce receives lifelong learning opportunities? Who pays for medical treatments in a healthier society? How a fairer economy pays its workers and prepares them to compete in the global economy? Whether building a national culture of service means a draft or incentivized service with subsidized college or graduate education or health care?

"Ideas have consequences," says columnist George F. Will, "large and lasting consequences."[1] What are the consequences of your idea? Anticipate the ideological, logistical, and budgetary consequences of your idea, such as the policy lines you would draw, how you would get your idea accomplished, and how you would pay for it and with whose money.

Assume that your vision is a safer America and your idea is to provide for the common defense through a strong military that will protect us from all enemies. Who is required or recruited or allowed to serve? How do you maintain force readiness and care for troops, military families, and veterans?

How much of the federal budget do you spend in relation to all the other needs of the country? Do you raise taxes, and, if so, whose?

Most important are the practical consequences: when and how do you propose to deploy the strong military to go to war and to protect us here at home?

WHAT ARE THE CORE VALUES
THAT SHAPE YOUR VISION AND IDEAS?

Just as integral to your vision of the future and your big ideas are the core values, such as equality, responsibility, and justice, that inspire you to achieve the vision. If your vision is of a safer America, and if your idea is to provide for the common defense through a strong military, your values will shape your treatment of the military servicemen and servicewomen. Equality shapes whom you call to serve: a draft or voluntary force; people from certain segments of society, or all people, regardless of race, gender, class, or sexual orientation. Responsibility shapes how you prepare them for missions against the real and immediate threats against our country and when you deploy them in harm's way at home or overseas. Justice guides whether you keep promises to military families and properly provide for veterans upon their return home.

TEST YOUR VISION, IDEAS, AND VALUES
TO SEE THE DIFFERENCE THEY MAKE
IN PEOPLE'S LIVES

So far we've been dealing with the imagination; your vision becomes real when you make choices in civic and political life that make a difference in people's lives.

On a personal level, you might achieve your vision for a safer America; your idea of a strong military; and your values of equality, responsibility, and justice by enlisting in the military or by supporting the families of people who enlist. On a community level, you might achieve the vision by supporting initiatives to provide workforce training and small-business loans to veterans returning home.

On a political level, you might volunteer to work for a candidate who shares your vision. How can you tell if a candidate shares your vision? Let's say, for example, that you were evaluating candidates for president, and several promise a vision of America with the idea of a strong military and the values of equality, responsibility, and justice. So far, so good, but who will achieve the vision in the manner you intend? Until a crisis brings it home, it's just a theory.

Consider this "NORAD test": Assume that, as happened on September 11, 2001,[2] it would take about seven minutes from the time that NORAD (the North American Aerospace Defense Command) gets word that the country is under attack to the time that fighter jets can be scrambled in response. If NORAD identifies a threat—a hijacked airplane or a missile over a U.S. population area—should the president order the jets to fire? At whom? With how many American lives at risk on the plane or on the ground?

Picture yourself or a loved one on the plane, in the targeted population area, or watching safe from immediate harm as the crisis unfolds. What do you want your president to do? What vision, ideas, and values do you want to see in the president who would have only those brief and critical seven minutes to make life-or-death decisions?

Although few other tests will be as dramatic, you need to articulate your vision for the future, your ideas and their

NANCY PELOSI

"Our diversity is our strength," says House Speaker Nancy Pelosi. Pelosi grew up in multiethnic Baltimore, where her call to service came as a young girl. Her family home was always open to constituents of her father, the late Mayor Thomas D'Alesandro Jr., and she attributes her call to service to her parents, who "raised us to be proud of our Italian Catholic heritage, patriotic in our love of country, and respectful of other people's pride in their heritage."

"When people ask me why I serve, I always answer in the same way: our children, our children, our children—the air they breathe, the water they drink, the food they eat, their health and education, a world at peace in which to live, the job security of their parents and the retirement security of their grandparents. I see my own service as an extension of my role as a mother of five and a grandmother of six." Before being elected as Speaker of the House of Representatives, she said: "When they hand me that gavel I will be receiving the gavel not just for the House Democrats but for all of America's children, because we have to answer to them, to make the future better for them."

Source: Nancy Pelosi, interview, July 14, 2007.

consequences, and the values that shape your call to service to see the difference they will make in people's lives.

BE PART OF SOMETHING
LARGER THAN YOURSELF

To experience the challenges and rewards of public service, and to find out what kind of engagement best suits your talents, work with people who share your vision, ideas, and values. Volunteer with a student organization, a community project, a nonprofit, or an election campaign. The way you act to achieve your vision is a signal to you and to others that you are engaged to *do* something: to make a difference in your community and make the future better.

"Know thy power," says House Speaker Nancy Pelosi. "Recognize your reponsibility to encourage other people who are on their own paths to public service. It is amazing how much you can accomplish if you are willing to share credit."[3] You must do something for people before you ask them to do something for you. Think of it this way: if you had a friend who showed up only when she needed something or called only to ask you for money, you would probably not stay friends for long. The same is true in public life. Don't be a taker. If someone gives you the opportunity to serve, pay it forward by helping someone else get involved or by donating money or resources to improve an organization.

Volunteer. "Every job I ever got I volunteered first," says Lezlee Westine, the CEO of TechNet, a bipartisan network of technology companies designed to promote innovation and competitiveness. "You cannot underestimate the huge value of volunteering for your first job. Volunteering is a great opportunity to show your passion for a cause and catapults you faster to a leadership role in an organization."[4]

Performing the basic tasks of campaigning—sorting mail, stuffing envelopes, answering phones—gives you hands-on experience. Your willingness to do the grunt work tests your commitment to a cause and demonstrates to you and to others that you are engaged to *do* something, not just to *be* something.

Register to vote. Literally dozens of elected officials who work for you at all levels of government are up for reelection every two, four, or six years. In addition, ballot measures at the local and possibly state levels are subject to voter approval. Be sure that you are registered to vote and that if you have moved, your registration is up to date. Being registered to vote is important for everyone, and it is critical for those considering a run for public office. Register other people to vote as well: encourage family and friends; register new citizens at their swearing-in ceremonies; participate in voter registration drives at fairs, festivals, and other community events.

If you see a workshop, take it. You will need to excel in the four metrics of public service: management, message, money, and mobilization. Try your hand at each one in order to develop your skills. There are many ways to learn the skills of democracy; for example, many local nonprofit organizations and political parties sponsor trainings for potential volunteers. Challenge yourself and develop your advocacy skills. Write letters to your local paper. Post a diary on your community blog. E-mail your elected officials. Prepare presentations and informational videos. Give progress reports to people you recruit to work with you, and develop your advocacy skills. Develop a network to continue the work you care about, and make a commitment to mentor people the way people mentored you.

Match your skills to a position. Certain skills sets are associated with particular types of public service positions: financial expertise for a nonprofit treasurer; advocacy skills for a legislator; executive experience for a potential mayor or board president. Volunteer in a nonprofit agency, work on a political campaign, or watch the city council or Congress in person or on public television to find a match between your skills and the work that interests you.

STRENGTHEN YOUR FRIENDSHIPS AND ALLIANCES IN NETWORKS

As you articulate your vision, ideas, and values; as you begin the service that puts them into action; and as you emerge as a trustworthy policy advocate, you will develop friendships and alliances.

Technology networks. TechNet's Lezlee Westine advises people to create technology networks through the Internet to organize local groups and individuals for fund-raising, communication with the public on a grassroots level without using traditional media, and targeting favorable voters for get-out-the-vote efforts.[5]

I saw many of these networks firsthand on the campaign trail in 2006. The top-down nature of institutions is being reinvigorated by the bottom-up rough and tumble of online social and political networking. This new blend of asymmetrical politics thrives on bringing old-school politics and new media together. In communities around the county, I visited with people who had lost confidence in the large institutions—such as government (because of Katrina, Iraq, and

LEZLEE WESTINE

Building opportunity through innovation and competitiveness inspires the service of Lezlee Westine, the chief executive officer of TechNet, a nonprofit bipartisan organization representing over a million employees in the fields of information technology, biotechnology, e-commerce, and finance. An expert in harnessing technology to improve people's everyday lives, Westine encourages aspiring public servants to do the same: "Build technology networks to bring people together, coalition networks to accomplish a policy goal, and human networks to advance and mentor other people."

Westine's call to service led her to Washington, D.C., where she worked from 2001 to 2005 in the George W. Bush White House as deputy assistant to the president and as director of the Office of Public Liaison. Working as the Bush administration's top liaison to the more than twenty thousand constituent and interest groups that interface with the White House each year, Westine built coalition networks for a variety of goals, including initiatives to support the 2001 economic package, to draw needed attention to the plight of Afghan women in the wake of September 11, and to increase funding for education programs. Now, through TechNet, Westine regularly engages a technology network of two hundred member companies in the political process. "Above all else, build connections and relationships—they are the glue that holds together any network."

Source: Lezlee Westine, interview, June 12, 2007.

corruption), corporations (due to Enron and other instances when executives bilked employees and investors), and churches (after the pedophilia scandals). Yet these people felt intense pride in their own community institutions and service traditions. Not only were they voting out a culture of corruption, they were ushering in a culture of service: walking precincts for candidates and walking 10k's for AIDS or breast cancer research; meeting to clean up politics and to clean up beaches, parks, and neighborhoods.

Coalition networks. Westine's service in the White House involved working with a series of coalition networks, which she describes as a "temporary alliance of groups to achieve a common goal." These coalition networks can include journalists, nongovernmental organizations, corporate executives, and political leaders—"groups of people with followings beyond themselves" organized around a specific policy objective.

Look for unlikely allies to join your coalition networks. Grassroots maven Dotty LeMieux, whose Green Dog Campaigns firm advises Northern California candidates and initiative campaigns, described a coalition to require that any new construction at the Marin County Civic Center be subject to a public vote. "A preservationist group attracted the interest of prison reformers (because a new jail was being contemplated at the site), anti-tax advocates (who feared being made to foot the bill for some lavish building projects), and neighbors (who wanted to keep things quiet)," she recalls. LeMieux and her unlikely allies sought endorsements from conservationist groups like the Sierra Club and social justice networks whose members joined their ranks as volunteer precinct workers, phone-bankers, and donors.[6]

Similarly, adds LeMieux, when plans were unveiled for a biotech medical research facility on one of the most visible hillsides in Marin County, a coalition was formed by many of these same groups. With the addition of animal rights activists (who opposed animal testing) and local service providers (who objected because community foundation funding for the facility would cut into their own resource pool), a referendum opposing the facility project passed easily. Conversely, an effort to stop a new golf course on the site of a historic blue oak forest failed because the developers were able to offer discount greens fees to local golfers, a community that outnumbered the environmentalists who led the opposition.

Human networks. The most effective way to build a culture of service is to develop a network of people who share your call to service. For example, your call to service may be the economic empowerment of women. A women's business network will help achieve the vision because it will do the following: host fund-raisers for women candidates or candidates who champion issues important to women; lobby government by showcasing the impact of woman-owned businesses in terms of numbers of workers and revenues; influence media coverage of the most powerful woman business owners; support women for political positions; and encourage successful women to mentor younger women. "From handshaking to supporting your peers to supporting a candidate, human networks will advance your goals and have untold benefits," advises Lezlee Westine.

Start building your human networks with the people whose leadership you admire. Work with a local nonprofit or political leader on a public service effort to learn the ropes, develop relationships, and take a shared risk.

Be part of a team. Networking requires you to work with and for other people. Politics and policy are about teamwork. Some people like to study, worship, and work alone; if you do, perhaps a behind-the-scenes role is appropriate for you. Assuming you enjoy the camaraderie and cooperation of a team effort, you will be spending most of your time asking other people to volunteer their time, write a check, bring their network in common cause with yours, and/or hire your candidate to work for them. If you decide to become a candidate or commissioner or nonprofit trustee, you will have a constituency to which you will have to answer, each of them with their own vote as to whether you can get the job, how you are doing in the job, and whether you should keep the job.

Finally, campaigns are environments where the stakes are high and the pressure is intense. Networking means listening, and the feedback you hear will not always be favorable. You will have to hear criticism about work that springs from your intensely personal core vision, ideas, and values—and not take it personally. Developing a thick skin is an integral part of your networking and public service experience.

PERFORM AN ACT OF COURAGE TO ACHIEVE YOUR VISION

The big test of your commitment to service will come when you have to risk your reputation and perform an act of courage to achieve your vision.

Meet people you don't know and ask them for help. Would you call someone you don't know to ask them to hire someone? Would you call up someone you don't know and ask them to hire you? Would you go to the home of someone you don't know, knock on the door, and ask them to hire you or a friend? Think of your last job interview. Now imagine giving it every day walking door-to-door in your neighborhood. Think of your last performance evaluation. Now imagine it posted on the Internet, with an opportunity for anyone to post their comments. That is a flavor of the exposure you have as a public leader. Your comfort level in talking to someone you don't know and receiving their feedback will reveal what sort of role you want to take, either behind the scenes, out front for a cause, or as a candidate yourself. The more dedicated you are to your cause, the easier it is to put yourself in the public eye and recruit support for your mission.

Challenge a sacred cow. Do you serve on the board of a nonprofit where the overhead seems excessive compared to the services performed? The sacred cow may be perks for the directors or money spent according to the whims of powerful donors rather than according to a mission statement. Do you live in a community where the government gives more benefits to corporations than it does to small businesses? The sacred cow may be a taxpayer benefit given to a powerful entity rather than to working people. Whatever your scope of service, identifying and tackling a sacred cow will require taking risks and leading on difficult issues.

Taking on sacred cows is especially important for women leaders. California political strategist Mary Hughes, whose "dream work" is helping women achieve power, says bipartisan public polling reveals that women face harsher scrutiny then men do with respect to their fiscal and national security credentials. To overcome this disadvantage, Hughes advises women to seek out opportunities to network in those circles by joining trade associations or policy forums that address those issues and to take on sacred cows in business practices and budgets.[7]

Take a political risk. You will face criticism and skepticism from people who think your ideas are unrealistic or politically impossible. That is to be expected. Working for a candidate running for office is always a risk. Although there are several people on the same ballot, only one person is going to win. If past experience shows that over 95 percent of incumbents are reelected, a challenger cannot expect to win and would be advised not to try. But dozens of Republicans beat the odds when running for Congress in 1994, as did dozens of Democrats running for Congress in 2006. Each made a personal decision to campaign for their vision, ideas, and values and risked losing to advance a service mission.

Demonstrating the courage of your convictions sometimes means you make the fight, even if you are not likely to win. The Fighting Dems numbered over fifty, with fewer than a dozen in statistically competitive districts. All the candidates and their supporters knew this from the start: they were running to show their vision for a strong America; their idea for a new direction for the war in Iraq; their values of duty, honor, and country. They risked their personal reputations, their finances, and their relationships with those in the military who would not oppose the commander in chief. Many of the candidates lost, but all of the campaigns succeeded in creating a drumbeat across America for a new direction in Iraq and for better care for troops and veterans.

GET YOUR POLICY ACT TOGETHER

All leaders must inspire trust. Before facing the public, you must know what you are talking about.

Research the duties and responsibilities of the position you seek. If you seek a leadership role in a nonprofit, labor union, business association, political campaign, or elective office, consider the prerequisites. Does the position require any particular credentials? Do you need a certified public accountant license or a law degree? Do you need ongoing professional education? If so, take care of business. If you are considering working for a government agency or elected official, look into the responsibilities to constituents, casework, and staffing requirements.

Master the public policy challenges. As you develop an understanding of the ideological, logistical, budgetary, and practical consequences of your own ideas, be sure to study "policy triggers"—the events or actions that affect laws. If you are gathering signatures for a ballot initiative, read the proposal first and be sure to understand what the law is now and how your measure will change it. Did you know that many states link some of their tax rates to federal tax rates? Check to see if your state does that before proposing a change in tax policy. One candidate did not check, and proposed a federal tax cut that—if passed—would have unbalanced his state budget by cutting the state rate and leaving the state budget in deficit. The governor was understandably displeased when called for comment. Another trigger to watch out for is the sunset date of any legislation: you don't want to get caught proposing a budget or law based on a provision that has expired.

Be knowledgeable and candid about the consequences of your proposals. Your word is your bond in politics. People have to trust you as an advocate. As a practical matter, your arguments are stronger if you can identify and counter the strongest arguments against them. As a personal matter, your integrity is underlined by your candor about the merits of your position versus the opposition. The late Jack Valenti—a decorated World War II combat pilot, Harvard MBA, White House speechwriter for President Lyndon B. Johnson, and longtime president of the Motion Picture Association of America—cautioned a bipartisan Capitol Hill audience: "Trust is everything." Valenti urged us to be honest about our ideas and candid about our opponents because, he said, "the people you are trying to influence will find out the merits of the other side eventually and will respect you all the more for being up front with them."[8]

Balance your purist and pragmatic tendencies. Do you see yourself as a purist or a pragmatist? How much of each? It might depend on the cause. Finding your balance with candor and clarity is essential to your success as people look to you for leadership. A purist can limit alliances or even discussions to like-minded people, but a pragmatist will have to reach across the spectrum of views to talk with everyone. Father Robert Drinan, a Catholic priest who served in Congress, was known as the consummate "pragmatic idealist" because he retained his core values yet moved beyond his own ideological circle to find new allies to advance his causes.

It helps to view policy through what Nancy Pelosi calls the "kaleidoscope" of politics. For example, when it comes to the environment, some of the same evangelicals and secular humanists who oppose each other with respect to the separation of church and state agree on the need to combat global warming, while some environmentalists and hunters who hold opposing views on gun control share a conservationist agenda to preserve natural resources. You never know where you might find common cause with people.

"Bush is right." A former Indiana congressman and member of the 9/11 Commission, Tim Roemer counsels aspiring pub-

FATHER ROBERT F. DRINAN

The ongoing responsibility to public service is embodied in the advice from the late congressman Father Robert F. Drinan to a group of his Georgetown University Law students: "As I look out at all of you with your new and expensive law school educations, I would urge you to go forth into society not as mere legal tradesmen, but as moral architects. Design, create, and build a better and more equitable society, and use your skills to help those who are otherwise not being served." Drinan agitated for justice for most of his eighty-six years. He was elected to Congress, where he served as chair of the Criminal Justice Subcommittee of the House Judiciary Committee and later opted to remain in the priesthood when the pope asked him to choose between his office and his ordination. Drinan's passion for justice included service in the law school classroom and the nonprofit boardroom, earning his peers' respect, with twenty-two honorary degrees as well as the 2004 American Bar Association Medal and the 2006 Congressional Distinguished Service Award, those institutions' highest honors. His final homily, delivered at the beginning of the 110th Congress in January 2007, was a powerful call to service seeking justice for the children of the world, particularly the children affected by Katrina and Darfur.

Source: Father Robert F. Drinan, remarks at mass honoring Speaker-elect Nancy Pelosi (Trinity University, Washington, D.C., January 3, 2007), http://www.trinitydc.edu/news_events/2007/012907_fr_drinan.php.

lic servants to find at least one issue on which to promote bipartisan solutions. In Roemer's current work, that issue is implementation of the unanimous, bipartisan 9/11 Commission reforms. No matter how much you disagree with people on the other side of the philosophical spectrum, counsels Roemer, there must be at least *one* issue on which you can work with the opposition to forge a constructive solution.[9]

For many progressives, "Bush is right" when it comes to the need to combat HIV/AIDS in Africa or genocide in Darfur. For many conservatives, "Nancy Pelosi is right" when it comes to veterans' rights, and "Harry Reid is right" when it comes to stem cell research. Your willingness to communicate the issues of a shared vision will demonstrate your maturity as a political thinker and as a public servant. If you are engaged in electoral politics, your success relies on a bipartisan vision for America on at least one issue; if you are in the nonprofit world, your tax-favored status depends on it.

In the words of former Congresswoman Lindy Boggs of Louisiana, "never fight each fight as if it were your last," because today's adversaries may well become tomorrow's allies. Your cause is bigger than your ego: no need to fight a scorched-earth battle only to wake up the next day needing grassroots support from former opponents for your venture.

WHAT DIFFERENCE WILL THIS MAKE?

After answering the call-to-service questions—"what is the vision?" "what are the ideas and their consequences?" "what values shape the policy?"—you come to the age-old question: "so what?"

What difference does this make? Every cycle, campaigners say, "This is the most important election in our lifetime." To them, perhaps. But to the voters? You have to let people know what difference you or your candidate would make in office. You have to explain why this race matters.

Explaining the difference a race makes is also important with ballot measures. Sometimes a public policy initiative comes on the ballot over and over again. In states like California, where the ballot initiative process allows just about anything to go before voters, it is assumed that legislative fights will carry over into the ballot box. A growth initiative goes from the voters to the county supervisors and back again. A reproductive choice question goes from ballot to ballot to ballot. A health care measure is passed by legislators, vetoed by the governor, and placed on the state ballot. And so forth.

This process grows tiresome for many voters, who feel as though they are doing the work they pay public officials to do. Your responsibility in presenting a ballot initiative is to explain to people why they should care.

One woman crystallized this sentiment to me during the 2005 campaign that successfully defeated a series of anti-worker ballot measures in California. I was phone-banking, and a woman I called told me how she had taken hours to read her voter handbook. She vented: "I send people to Sacramento to do this kind of work. Besides, it takes a PhD to figure these things out—I *have* a PhD, so I *can* figure it out, but *why should I have to?*" Why, indeed. I thanked her for her "no" vote, and told her story during the rest of my phone-banking to urge more "no" votes.

But when the shoe is on the other foot and you seek a "yes" vote on an initiative, the burden will be on you to lay out the urgency of the situation, the policy implications of the initiative, and the practical consequences of doing nothing.

Before supporting a candidate or ballot measure, be sure you know why this race matters: why this person has to be

elected right now or why this measure has to be approved
by the voters; what exactly the candidate or initiative will
accomplish for people; and how this measure achieves the
vision, ideas, and values that call you to service.

CONSIDER THE UNWELCOME SURPRISES

Whenever you are seeking support of others to gain a high-
profile position, everything you have said or done can be
trumpeted across the *New York Times* or a local blog. In
today's Internet era, your life is an open Facebook. Be prepared by being honest and keeping a sense of perspective.

A classic axiom of public life is, "You can go to church to
confess your sins, or you can go into politics and have your
opponents confess them for you."

Consider your personal, financial, political, or criminal
background, ranging from every address, job, and position
you have held to any civil or criminal proceedings in which
you have been involved. Remember the Rule of One—
everyone tells someone. A friend told me that he once asked
a prominent official about a sensitive matter. "I trust you,"
the official responded, "but I'm not sure I can trust the person you're going to tell." It's human nature—neither lips
nor records stay sealed.

In most community organizations, you have to complete a
background check in order to serve on a nonprofit board of
directors. Be sure that your résumé is accurate, your credentials are in order, and you are prepared to explain any past
mistakes that may come up. Most of all, be sure you have
lived up to the standards you set for others. If you preach
family values, live them. If you seek forgiveness for your
mistakes, offer it to others in personal and public life. Nothing stings more sharply than hypocrisy.

People competing for the same job—on a board or for a political office—or those who are opposed to your service mission may link your "minor," "distant," "remote," "forgotten," "childish," "foolish," "rash," "youthful" "young and irresponsible" acts together in order to gain competitive advantage. The more sacred cows you tackle, the more someone who is threatened by change may want to sideline you. So you have to ask the hard questions about yourself.

Consider the answers you would owe to your spouse, your children, your friends, your supporters, the press, and the media when the skeletons tumble out of the closet. What can you do? Take an inventory of your life, and review it with your circle of trusted advisers. Then remember: no one lives a sainted life. Everyone makes mistakes; people generally care less that you made mistakes than they do that you dealt with them properly. The American people are forgiving and compassionate. If you can express a lesson learned and demonstrate that you have earned the trust and support of others—particularly those who may have been aggrieved by your actions—you have the opportunity to place events in perspective and continue with your service.

MAKE A PERSONAL COMMITMENT TO SERVICE

Once you identify the vision, ideas, and values that call you to service; volunteer for causes and/or candidates; take risks; establish friendships; engage in social networking; and consider the unwelcome surprises, you are ready to decide what kind of personal service is best for you and your family.

Start with your family. Everyone has to balance the needs of family and work. This balance is impossible in politics unless your family is committed to your goal. You can dedicate sixteen-hour days to the startup work of a nonprofit, political cause, or election campaign only if your loved ones support your desire to devote your—and their—time, energy, resources, and reputation to public service.

Your time and energy devoted to a cause is time and energy away from Little League, book clubs, grocery shopping, and helping with homework. Build time into your family schedule for volunteering and service along with these other family activities. If you're at community meetings or serving in office, who's watching the kids, picking up the groceries, and preparing the meals?

Your resources include your own funds: you may need to take a leave from your job or curtail your work hours. Can you invest 5 to 10 percent of your disposable income, take out a loan, mortgage your home, give up cable TV, and put thousands of miles on the family car? Jan Brown describes the commitment that she and her husband, Fighting Dem Charlie Brown, made when committing to his campaign for Congress in 2006 this way: "We cancelled our cable TV subscription, drove thousands of miles to each and every community in our rural district, and devoted all our spare time to the campaign so we could call attention to a new direction for the Iraq war, for our son Jeff who is serving, and for all the servicemembers and their families." The Browns even spent their 2006 wedding anniversary campaigning at a Nevada City house meeting. "Once we arrived and were getting out of the car, the campaign manager managed to close the trunk on my right hand," remembers Jan Brown. After bandaging her bleeding hand, Jan went to the party, made the "ask" for donations and volunteers, and tried to avoid shaking hands that night. "An anniversary to remember," she concludes. "Nothing is going to stop us when we are campaigning, nothing, it is too important."[10] This is not the way most of us would want to spend a romantic anniversary, but the Browns made the choice to honor their service mission. Campaigning is a marathon that takes a personal and financial toll: be sure your family is ready to pay it.

Your reputation is not individual; it includes your partner, spouse, kids, parents, and close friends who will lose some of their privacy. Your family and friends will also have to live with you if you win—and if you lose. All of this must factor into your decision. Explain your call to service, the nature of your mission, and the campaigning you may ask of them. Be clear about their roles in any public efforts. Be ready to take a risk together: you may put your family time, energy, resources, and reputation on the line, work your heart out, and lose. If so, what then? Before you embark on this family commitment, be sure you reach a family decision.

Once you take everything into account and decide to go ahead, you are ready to take the leap onto a public stage.

You may decide to lead a nonprofit service agency. You may choose to accept a public trust position as an appointed official—city commissioner, deputy prosecutor, or county administrator. You may decide to chair a ballot initiative campaign. You may assume leadership in a political campaign. You may decide to run for office yourself.

"Consider yourself asked." You may be thinking about running for office and feel confident about your commitment to serve but are unsure about whether you can win. This feeling is particularly true for women, according to a 2004 Brown University report that asked, "Why Don't Women Run for Office?" The researchers found that women are less likely than men to have received the suggestion to run for office from party and elected officials, political activists, or family and friends; yet when women receive external support from

formal and informal political and nonpolitical sources, they are twice as likely to run.[11] Ellen Malcolm, founder of EMILY's List, a national network of 100,000 members who recruit, train, and support Democratic pro-choice women candidates, says the Brown study shows that people who care about public service should encourage others to run. The theory behind EMILY's List—*EMILY* stands for Early Money Is Like Yeast—is that early networking and institutional support helps the campaign "dough" rise. Malcolm says establishing a pipeline for women to run is essential because "progress doesn't happen in a moment, but in battle after battle for our values."

Malcolm's message to potential candidates: "Consider yourself asked."[15]

GET REAL:
TAKE THE PUBLIC SERVICE FITNESS TEST

1. **What is your vision for the future that calls you to service?**

   If you had the power to change the world, what would the future be like? Consider the actions you have taken in your community—with nonprofits, local organizations, and/or political campaigns. What kind of future are you trying to build for future generations?

2. **What is the bold stroke—your big idea—to achieve your vision?**

   What are the consequences of your idea? What are the ideological, logistical, and budgetary consequences of your idea: what policy lines would you draw; how would you accomplish your ideas, and, how would you pay for it and with whose money?

3. **What are the core values that shape your vision and ideas?**

   What do you believe? What are the values that shape how you see the world and how you would achieve your vision?

4. **Do you want to do something or to be something?**

   What is your volunteer history? Are you involved because you really want to work for people or are you in it for ego, power, money, or fame? Who have you actively encouraged, supported, or mentored in their path to public service?

5. **What act of political courage have you taken to achieve your vision?**

   What risk have you taken for causes and candidates? Did you challenge a sacred cow?

6. **Do you have public service credentials?**

   What have you done for people? Do people trust you to make a difference for the cause? Do you understand what the position demands, and are you prepared to meet those demands? Can you ask thousands of people you don't know to give you a job or give money to your cause?

7. **Have you made friends and established alliances?**

   Whom do you admire in your personal life? Who are your political heroes? What service have you performed with, or in networks related to, the work of your personal or political heroes? Have you built the technology, coalition, and human networks to succeed? Are the networks prepared to support you, your cause, or your candidate with time, energy, and resources?

8. What difference does this service make?

Why does th'is service matter? Why should people care about your cause or candidate?

9. How do you handle crisis and criticism?

How do you handle criticism about work that springs from your core vision, ideas, and values? When conditions get chaotic, what is your temperament?

10. Are you carrying any personal or political baggage?

Have you supported controversial candidates or political organizations? Is there something in your past that you need to reconcile or explain? How will you deal with this?

11. Is your family ready for you to serve?

Do your loved ones support your desire to devote your time, energy, resources, and reputation to public service? If you are taking a lead role in a campaign as a manager or candidate, does your family know that they will not see you very often during the campaign, which may last a year or two? Are they committed to your goal? Will they offer you support and campaign with you?

12. Are you personally committed to serve?

Do you want to run for office? Are you ready for a marathon? Can you take a leave from work? If you are running a campaign or offering yourself as a candidate, will you take out a loan or mortgage your home to win if need be? Consider your biggest disappointment. Now magnify it on a public scale. If you put all your time, energy, and effort into a public service campaign, work your heart out and lose, what then?

TWO

Know Your Community

Boston's three favorite pastimes are politics, sports,
and revenge. —*Anonymous*

The old adage about Boston can be applied to nearly any
neighborhood in America: every community has its unique
way of life, a political and cultural history that you need to
learn to serve effectively. You must know your neighbors
and their families: how they live, work, worship, and recreate
and their hopes, dreams, and aspirations for their kids and
their parents. And, of course, their baseball teams.

As you prepare to serve your community as a volunteer
for a cause or as a candidate for office, prepare, connect, and
target: First, prepare a community inventory to gather raw
data about the people, the geography, the traditions, the opinion leaders, the politics, and the technology, coalition, and
human networks. Second, connect with the community leaders and organizations that enhance civic life. Third, target
people who are likely to support your candidate or cause.

PREPARE A COMMUNITY INVENTORY

The people. To get to know the people in your community,
start with a broad view. Look up the national census data and

local sources of demographic data, which will tell you about the number of people overall; the breakdown in terms of age, gender, ethnicity, and family units. Look up the ethnic composition of the community. Break down the voting population by age, highlighting seniors, people drawing social security, and families with children.

Then look at how people live: Do they rent or own their homes? What is the per capita income? How does the per capita income vary by neighborhood? Where do the children and young people and adults go to elementary school, college, or vocational school? Know the local economy, particularly the largest employers in each of the private, public, and nonprofit sectors. What are the fastest-growing industries for jobs, and what are the small-business opportunities?

The geography. Once you get a handle on the raw population data, you can literally map out your community, be it urban, suburban, rural, or a combination. Start with physical maps. "Maps tell you about the territory," says political strategist Mary Hughes. She encourages aspiring public servants to collect as many maps as possible of parkland, transit routes, political districts, schools, population and growth centers, real estate (available commercial space), historical museums, and landmarks. "You don't know your community until you know these basics," Hughes advises.[1]

The traditions. Every community has traditions that shape the local culture: the Big Game, annual neighborhood or ethnic festivals, Fourth of July parades, chamber picnics, beach cleanups, walkathons, and 5k races. Each of these events is made possible through the support of community leaders— block club presidents, church deacons, shop stewards, and parent-teacher association (PTA) officers—who bring other people together to participate in these traditions. For example, PTA officers are some of the best-organized community leaders: they are part of an academic community for over ten years while their kids grow up, and they are networking constantly with other parents and teachers, so they have their fingers on the pulse of the community.

The opinion leaders. Every community has its icons: people who command respect through their outstanding achievement in political, business, cultural, or philanthropic endeavors. In addition, there are opinion leaders (newspaper columnists, philanthropists, labor leaders, corporate leaders, nonprofit directors, civil rights and human rights organizers) and people connected with cultural landmarks, places of worship, and institutions held in high regard, such as universities, think tanks, foundations, civic organizations, and business associations. Through local news outlets, yellow pages searches, and online searches, you can identify the traditions, their sponsors, and their supporters. Two other good sources of community opinion leaders are the local and ethnic chambers of commerce and the cadre of appointed city or county commissioners, as these are emerging leaders at the crossroads of government, business, culture, and philanthropy.

The challenges. Gerald W. McEntee, president of AFSCME, expects aspiring leaders to know "the hopes and the challenges of the people in your community. More than being aware of problems in your district, you need to care about people's challenges and have a way to help solve them," he says.[2]

The politics. If you are looking for support for a cause or candidate, consider the political habits of your community in order to assess your chances of success. Start by looking up how many people are eligible, registered, and voting. Look at voter registration figures and election results from your secretary of state or county elections official to see how many people were registered and voted in recent elections. If you are considering running for election as a Democrat or Republican, or working for a Democratic or Republican candidate, the party registration will give you an idea as to whether you can win. If the numbers are not in your favor, consider whether you have the resources to register enough new voters or persuade enough voters to cross party lines to support you or your candidate. You should also take a look at independent voters as well as whether significant races (such as the presidential race or ballot initiatives) or highly competitive local races will be on the ballot because these contests historically bring more voters to the polls.

If you are working for a candidate, voters will expect to know that person's vision, big idea, acts of political courage, service credentials, and experience. Independent voters in states that allow party registration have already made a decision: they have opted not to register with a particular political party. Political party registrations give you a starting point, but you have to look beyond party labels for all voters to discern their concerns value by value and priority by priority. Election results for ballot initiatives relating to taxes, growth, school bonds, library bonds, labor relations, and social issues may reveal voters' values and the priorities that those values represent. After a review of the voting patterns, consider whether there is a deciding voting bloc that can determine the outcome of the election.

Logistically, you should know how the people vote, what sorts of election technology they use, and whether they vote early, by absentee ballot, or by mail. If most people vote

GERALD McENTEE

For Gerald McEntee, union organizing began in the family. His father was a trash truck driver in Philadelphia, rising to be a union steward, business agent, and head of the local council before being elected vice president of AFSCME. His childhood memories include his dad on the phone all night listening to grievances and trying to solve problems. After serving in the army, McEntee went to work as an organizer and led a campaign to attain collective bargaining rights in Pennsylvania. He rose to head the state union and then served as his father had as international vice president of AFSCME before being elected president of the union and its 1.4 million public service employees.

What motivates McEntee as he nears his fiftieth anniversary in the public service employee union and twenty-fifth year as its president? It is the unfinished business of helping working families, including "our child care workers and home health care workers." AFSCME established candidate boot camps because, McEntee explains, politics and organizing are "joined at the hip. Our members are concerned about the war in Iraq, health care, and retirement security—questions that must be answered at the federal level—and we want to make sure candidates are prepared to address them with honesty, vision, a mind and a heart that automatically go to the problems of working people, and a plan to win." McEntee is still inspired by memories of his father on the phone working out problems and expects public officials to do the same for their people: "to be aware of the existence of problems in their district, to have a bond with people, and to work toward solutions."

Source: Gerald W. McEntee, interview, April 25, 2007.

early, for example, you will want to begin your outreach earlier and plan from the beginning to ask your election protection team (see chapter 3, Build Your Leadership Teams, for more on election protection teams) to develop an early-voting campaign strategy.

Also consider the people elected at the local, county, state, and federal levels. To be effective, you need the support of others who have served before you. Review your relationships with the people elected to represent your community at the local, county, state, and federal levels. Consider also the various political camps in your community, and who is on which side. Will you be forced to choose sides, and if so which side shares your values? Have you worked for or against the election of any of these people? Did everyone come together after the last fight, or do you have some fence-mending to do? Which of these elected officials and political leaders are likely to get involved in your cause or campaign?

The technology, coalition, and human networks. Many community traditions and political actions are perpetuated through the work of technology networks. As discussed in chapter 1, Identify Your Call to Service, there are technology networks, coalition networks, and human networks that you may have developed through your own public service. Now you can use those networks to identify others. Not only can you tap into your own networks but you can ask your network partners to provide you with information about events and issues.

This drawing on networks includes outreach to the netroots—Internet-savvy, politically oriented community leaders, many of whom joined forces during the 2004 presidential campaign and stayed together to work on political and civic service efforts.

For example, the Howard Dean for president campaign effort attracted tens of thousands of volunteers who remain actively involved in the campaign's legacy organization, Democracy for America (DFA), which engages in ongoing grassroots trainings and public service advocacy. Will Easton, a longtime DFA volunteer, describes how the San Francisco DFA chapter stays together: "We were all volunteering so much time for voter registration, get-out-the-vote activities, and the like, that it seemed natural to volunteer just a little more time to do some community service work." The Dean volunteers decided to work with a local food bank and a park's native species replantings program, and to identify special projects such as beach cleanups, public television pledge drives, and provision of phone cards for veterans.

From the 2004 elections emerged good friendships among a critical mass of people interested in politics and community service as well as core teams willing to take on leadership functions, so they just kept right on going with monthly meetings and other activities. Easton asserts: "There's a critical role for groups like ours to play in grassroots politics—helping get more people involved in the process, not just in terms of voting but also in connecting with campaigns and issues where they want to make a difference." To identify networking leaders, start with the online networking sites—Facebook, MySpace, Friendster, LinkedIn, and other networking sites—with members in your community. Establish a presence on those sites, advises Easton, and ask people to show up for real-world events and meet one another face-to-face.[3]

Include outreach to the technology networks that have arisen among the new generation of veterans. "Political and civic leaders should reach out to the military, both to nearby bases and to veterans in their communities, to involve them in public life," advises Iraq and Afghanistan Veterans of America (IAVA) member Phillip Carter.[4] VoteVets.org and IAVA (www.iava.org) have organized messaging around national security and veterans' issues. These veterans-based networks focus on logistical support for servicemembers and their families, as well as physical and mental health care and job assistance for returning veterans.

Another veterans network is the Colorado Veterans for America (CVA), a group of veterans and members of military families with a shared mission to elect leaders who support veterans and active duty, National Guard, and Reserve personnel and their families. In October 2006 CVA member Mick Bilney told me that with over three thousand members across the state, and over one thousand people signed up to work in the highly contested Seventh Congressional District, veterans issues would be a major theme in outreach to Democrats and Independents.

National networks. On a broader level there are national grassroots organizations with local chapters whose memberships include emerging political leaders. The largest online community is MoveOn.org, which began as an online petition to censure and move on during the Clinton impeachment saga and now boasts 3.3 million members, who organize in all fifty states through Web-based e-mail alerts, house meetings, phone banks, and grassroots events. MoveOn's cofounder, Joan Blades, went on to found another organization, MomsRising.org, and in 2007 added men to the mix with FamiliesRising.org.

On the conservative side, RightMarch.com boasts over a million members. The Club for Growth has risen to prominence advocating policy goals such as making the Bush tax cuts permanent, cutting and limiting government spending,

CALL TO SERVICE
PHILLIP CARTER

A new generation is heeding the call to "provide for the common defense." Iraq and Afghanistan Veterans of America advocate Phillip Carter says he joined the Army Reserve Officer Training Corps (ROTC) program at UCLA "because I wanted a challenging job after graduation, and also because ROTC offered to pay for my last two years of college. I chose to be a military police lieutenant after college because I wanted to be on the front lines of our peacekeeping efforts in the Balkans." Explains Carter, "I got a lot more out of my military experience than just two years of tuition. I learned from my soldiers, who comprised a cross-section of American society [and] I learned a great deal about the practical aspects of American foreign policy, from establishing a checkpoint on a busy highway in South Korea to advising the police and courts in Baqubah, Iraq."

Carter is part of a new generation of veterans' advocates who are holding Democrats and Republicans accountable to military families. Noting that less than 1 percent of Americans—and less than 3 percent of our draft-age population—serves today in uniform, Carter warns: "There is a deep civil-military divide, which is dangerous for the health and future of our democracy. As a veteran, I believe I have the duty to bridge this civil-military divide through my writing on national security issues, and also through my advocacy work for IAVA. Even though I don't wear the uniform any longer, I still feel a strong obligation to serve in these ways and will likely do so for the rest of my life."

Source: Phillip Carter, e-mail, May 24, 2007.

creating personal retirement accounts in Social Security, expanding free trade, and allowing school choice. The organization is particularly active in identifying candidates and messages in Republican primaries.[5]

Each of these national organizations has local leaders who have engaged in various political and community campaigns. You can visit the sites and enter your zip code to find events in your community. These organizations often form coalition networks around particular issues such as Iraq, energy, taxes, and net neutrality.

Campus networks. Outreach to young people is especially critical. Nearly every community has a college, and nearly every college has a tradition of student activism, including local chapters of national organizations. Many of these organizations have years of experience in developing young leadership. If you are seeking progressive volunteers, you might look for College Democrats or progressive campus networks such as the women's rights, environmental, Public Interest Research Group, and ethnic organizations, and lesbian, gay, bisexual, and transgender (LGBT) pride chapters. If you are seeking conservative volunteers, check to see if there are local chapters of College Republicans or conservative campus networks such as the Intercollegiate Studies Institute (ISI), the Collegiate Network, the Leadership Institute, Young America's Foundation, or the Heritage Foundation. Consider groups that reach across the political spectrum to organize around causes. For example, young Americans from a variety of political and religious traditions are asserting leadership on the cause of combating genocide in the Sudan. Web sites like SaveDarfur.org and RocktheVote.org list local Divest for Darfur chapters. Log on to see if there are any chapters in your area.

Outreach to college students should start where they are and start when they start. Have a plan for the week before classes start. Be prepared to staff a table the first two weeks of class every semester. Recruit young people to lead the effort, give them training, help them write a plan, and coach them to be competent civic activists.

Youth networks. A Greenberg & Associates poll released in April 2007 demonstrates the power of the youth vote: "1.5 million more young people [voters under thirty] turned out to vote in 2006 than in 2004. Most of the contact with young voters (and potential voters) in 2006 came from nonpartisan, nonprofit organizations who worked out in the field." Effective outreach "reaches them where they are—on the Web, via text messaging—addresses and produces on the issues they care about, and approaches them in an authentic style they can relate to, [to forge] a significant and lifelong relationship."[6] Pollster Celinda Lake expects young voters to be a battleground constituency in 2008. "Research demonstrates that people who vote the same way three times in a row tend to vote that way disproportionately over the rest of their lifetime."[7] With young people having voted twice for Democrats, in 2004 and 2006, anticipate that Democrats will try to seal the deal in 2008, while Republicans will try to break the pattern.

NETWORK WITH COMMUNITY SERVICE LEADERS

Now that you have identified the people, geography, traditions, opinion leaders, politics, and online networks relevant to your campaign or candidate, it is time to connect with them. Start with the groups that are doing work that appeals to your personal call to service.

If you are thinking of running for office or accepting a leadership position with a communitywide nonprofit agency, get out and visit. Candidates for office or organizers embarking on a public service mission are well advised to begin with a listening tour, where they can meet people and hear their concerns.

No one expects you to make up for a lifetime in a few months; however, people do expect that if you are going to lead, you will begin by showing your respect for them.

An example of how to show your respect for the people and traditions of your community is Congressman Bruce Braley's work in Iowa's First Congressional District. This was an open seat with no incumbent and no clear advantage in voter registration for either political party. Braley made a commitment to represent everyone in the district, no matter their political party, and set out to visit with as many people as possible. Braley posted a map of all twelve counties on his Web site so people could click on the county for a schedule of events, which ranged from meet and greets to town hall forums to steak fries and pork chop dinners to 5k runs and homecoming parades.

Braley's August 2006 tour of Mississippi River towns along and near the Great River Road National Scenic Byway included the following: a stop at the town gazebo in Guttenberg; a film screening at the Field of Dreams Movie Site in Dyersville; a meet and greet at the Port of Dubuque; a tour of the Young Historical Museum in Bellevue; a barbeque in Clinton; events at the Tug Fest and the Buffalo Bill Museum in Le Claire; and an Ice Cream Social in Centennial Park in downtown Davenport, Iowa. By the time his tour was finished, Braley had a deeper respect for the traditions and a broader knowledge of the values and issues in the campaign.

The people, in turn, had his visits to their neighborhoods and his articulation of their concerns as proof that he saw them as his future employers. [8]

Like Congressman Braley, you need to get out and visit with people in order to understand their aspirations. Be sure to keep in contact with the people you meet, adding them to your technology, coalition, and human networks as appropriate. Ongoing updates will let you know what concerns are foremost in people's minds as well as the fund-raising and organizational work they are doing.

If you are working with an incumbent, keep visiting with people as aggressively as you did when the person was a candidate first seeking the job. By all means, don't stop listening. Many newly elected party and public officials embark on thank-you tours when they are elected, and listening sessions once they are in office, to stay close.

If you are working for a public servant or are an incumbent yourself, help the other members of your community's official family. Congressman Mike Thompson, Democrat of California, a leader of the Blue Dog Coalition, says it is essential to stay close to your official family of elected officials. Thompson plans an annual event for the elected officials and community leaders in each county of his sprawling north coast California congressional district. This is one of the many ways in which he tours his district, listens to people's concerns, and goes to them rather than waiting for them to come to him.[9]

TAKE A VIRTUAL TOUR OF
YOUR ONLINE COMMUNITIES

Just like the physical tour of your geographical community, take a virtual tour of your online communities. The protocols are similar: you need campaign ambassadors to make the introductions, and you need to listen before you speak. Campaigns' failure to listen is a pet peeve of online community leaders. Nothing alienates potential online allies faster than blanket requests for support or cash.

Start by understanding your audience. *Daily Kos* founder Markos Moulitsas describes his blog as "one of dozens of online communities, all of them focused on specific issues. It's a big ecosystem, and each site plays its role, sometimes overlapping efforts, but otherwise focusing attention and energy on action." Moulitsas advises public service campaigns to know each individual community: "They all have different focuses, different cultures, and different personalities. One blog or community is not like any other." Because *Daily Kos* is focused mostly on elections and Iraq, and has a national (not local) scope, your outreach and outreach must reflect that.[10] "Know whether a site's culture revolves around a high-profile lead blogger, or whether it's a more community-minded approach," says Moulitsas. "[For instance,] *Eschaton* [www.atrios.blogspot.com] is a site heavily dominated by its lead blogger's (Atrios's) voice. *Daily Kos*, on the other hand, is a cacophony of voices, each doing its own thing without my involvement. So if you want to reach the *Eschaton* community, you likely have to go through Atrios. But if you want to reach the *Daily Kos* community, you can use the diaries function to interact directly with that community without ever involving me." This means that you should create an account, write up a diary, and respond when comments are made to your diaries.

Be advised that online communities are not dumping grounds for press releases; rather, they are places to engage in conversations. "If you want to come and have a chat, then most online communities will give you a fair hearing. If you come in trying to market to them, they'll turn on you with a vengeance," Moulitsas warns. "Realize that you aren't the only person, campaign, or operation with an important mission." Rather than expecting people to embrace you just because you're doing "good" or "important" work, Moulitsas advises, "give people a reason to get excited about your efforts and don't assume or expect anything."[11]

Friend-raising comes before fund-raising. If at all possible, your campaign should be making informational communications to make friends (friend-raising) before sending contribution solicitations (fund-raising). This is particularly true with online communities. The order is so significant to so many people that I opted to place the advice here in chapter 2, Know Your Community, rather than in chapter 6, Raise the Money, although we will certainly revisit the topic in the online fund-raising section.

Consider these words of wisdom from Democratic netroots guru Tim Tagaris, currently Internet coordinator for Chris Dodd's presidential campaign, whose Web post of December 2004 on the netroots became an instant classic. Tagaris wrote: "If you want to withdraw cash using my ATM card (and millions like me), if you want to build that 'political movement' on-line, you better know the pin number."[12] The 4-digit pin number Tagaris identifies (see the box on page 50): first, direct communication with online communities; second, involving netroots in your effort; third, outreach to opinion leaders; and, fourth, your position on the issues/your opponent.

The essence of online networking is summarized by Tagaris's observation that "the ideas of 50,000 [people] will almost always be better than the ideas of 5 people who live their entire lives inside of a campaign headquarters." You have to let go some control and listen to the wisdom of crowds if you are going to represent people or attract large numbers of them to your cause.

TARGET YOUR SUPPORTERS

To determine whether your cause or candidate can succeed, take a look at different groups of people and target the folks whose support you need.

Software programs will allow you to create categories of information and merge them into a master file. Many candidates and ballot initiative campaigns will purchase a voter file from election officials. If you are working with a nonprofit organization, you will likely have a list of names, addresses, phone numbers, e-mail addresses, and participation histories. A voter file works essentially the same way—a public Rolodex telling you who is registered, whether they are registered with a political party, where they live, and how often they vote. (If you are lucky it may also have e-mail addresses and telephone numbers.) Voters are organized by small geographical units covering a few city blocks or county roads called *precincts*, each of which includes about a thousand voters according to a 2004 U.S. Election Assistance Commission survey.

Take this list of voters in each precinct of the area you want to cover and cross-check it with your community inventory data—people, geography, traditions, leaders, politics, and networks. Merge the file with commercially available consumer information, personal Rolodexes, membership lists, and input from individual volunteers who have reached these voters directly.

Let's say you are organizing support for a ballot initiative to promote after-school programs. One strategy is to reach

TIM TAGARIS:
"IF YOU WANT TO USE MY ATM CARD,
YOU BETTER KNOW MY PIN NUMBER"

First Number: Be willing to communicate with us. If you want that first digit you need to be willing to communicate with us, directly. . . . Yes, all campaigns should have [an Internet coordinator with] a seat at the table. . . . The Internet is the only medium available that allows for mass two-way communication. . . . Constituents want to . . . know what is going on in the campaign they are supporting. . . . They deserve it. That means you have a blog affiliated with your campaign, and the candidate posts on it, the campaign manager posts on it, etc. . . . in a "human voice." . . . Think outside the webpage. There are already communities that have hundreds, thousands, and hundreds of thousands of members. . . . And dammit, every communication should not include a link to your contribution page.

Second Number: We want to be involved in the effort. And more involved than just, "hey we need 4,000 literature pieces for the county fair coming up." Sure, it is nice to know what our money is going towards, but we want some form of "ownership" of the effort. That means soliciting our ideas and implementing the best of them. The ideas of 50,000 will almost always be better than the ideas of five people who live their entire lives inside of a campaign [headquarters]. Give them the tools to throw a house party, create a .pdf file for the campaign, listen to them about your message and refine it when necessary. Take one of the biggest successes of the Jeff Seemann for

Congress campaign, "campaign manager for a day." It was a media bonanza for us, fundraising success, it built our email list, drove people to our website in unheard of numbers for a congressional race, and most importantly, got people very excited about our effort in the 16th district of Ohio. . . .

Third Number: Opinion Leaders. Online is no different than off-line in this respect. There are certain opinion leaders that carry a lot of sway within a community, the Net is no different. The best of them understand quite well when someone is just trying to cash in on the netroots and who really "gets it." If you think you are going to pull a fast one on them and use them for the supporters, think again. Reach out to them. With the netroots ATM card . . .the opinion leader concept and two-step flow of communication theory holds true just as well online as it does off.

Fourth Number: Your positions on the issues/your opponent. If you are a progressive candidate, you are at an advantage on-line. . . . Yes, it helps if you have a bad opponent. . . .

Bottom line: It isn't fundraising requests that breed successful netroots fundraising. I would even venture to say that the fundraising application isn't the most important of the potential uses of the Internet. Unfortunately, right now it's the language that most everybody outside of the netroots speaks in.

Source: Tim Tagaris, e-mail, June 2, 2007; "My ATM Pin Number—Or Fundraising On-line," MyDD blog, December 23, 2004, http://www.mydd.com/story/2004/12/23/114450/18.

out to the PTA officers and child advocacy groups in your community and invite people to share their personal Rolodexes and organizational membership lists so you have a list of potential allies to target. Then cross-check these names against the voter files in your precincts to see who is registered and voting, who needs to update their registration, and who needs to become registered.

Once targets are identified, the people making peer-to-peer contact can ask for people's support and include specific information on where to register to vote if necessary. If voters express support for your cause or candidate, update your file. If allies register to vote or update their registration, be sure that your file reflects that and that the registrar of voters provides you with an updated list.

The gold standard in this area is the Republicans' national Voter Vault, which compiles information on targeted voters, sends it out to competitive races across the country, and monitors the results of its use over time. This process culminates in the last weekend before Election Day in the "72-Hour Plan" of voter contact in the final three days before the polls close. To this end, longtime Republican presidential adviser Karl Rove has trumpeted the use of "microtargeting" through databases and search tools used to divide voters by their backgrounds and interests, appeal to them with tailored pitches, identify sympathetic voters, and try to move them to the polls.

The Republican National Committee uses the Voter Vault database to identify voters with labels showing what issues would likely persuade them to vote Republican so that people can call or visit these voters to encourage them to vote. A published report from November 2006 indicates that Republican Party leaders put over $15 million into the system to generate an estimated twenty-four million telephone calls or in-person contacts to conservative voters.[13]

This new technology adds efficiency to what used to be a time-intensive process. During the 1987 Nancy Pelosi for Congress campaign, my mom deployed the Nana Brigade— my Italian grandmother and her friends sending postcards to their neighbors with Italian surnames urging them to vote. Our Nana Brigade sat around a dining room table using yellow highlighter pens to mark Italian surnames on the voter file printouts, and then handwrote the postcards.

Nowadays, the Nana Brigade meets Karl Rove. Rather than have the nanas highlight the names themselves from the voter rolls, some of this cross-checking can be done electronically (by ordering a batch of voters with certain Italian surnames from the voter file, adding names of Italian organization members, and putting in commercial data such as lists of people who subscribe to Italian newspapers or magazines), leaving more time for the handwritten postcards. Same outreach, new technology.

The science of targeting numbers will always need the art of local wisdom. Microtargeting only works with input from people on the ground, in the communities. A classic cautionary tale comes from Democratic strategist Donnie Fowler, who has worked in the field on every presidential campaign since 1988. Fowler recounted a story he heard when he first arrived in Iowa for the presidential caucuses: "A candidate preparing to broadcast a pro-choice message thought he had a receptive audience in an eastern Iowa community full of single women Democratic voters . . . until a closer look revealed that the precinct was a convent full of nuns."[14]

Although the nuns will know that your candidate is prochoice—as would anyone reading your campaign Web site—targeting them with a pro-choice message will reflect badly on your campaign. The lesson, says Fowler, is that even if a high percentage of people agree with your position on an issue, your campaign is wasting resources by broadcasting the same message to 100 percent of them. You have to narrowcast, based on input from people on the ground. In the nuns' case, this input saved the candidate major embarrassment. Fowler concludes: "Campaigning is an art and a science—the science is the data, and the art is the local wisdom."[15]

GUT CHECK:
CAN YOU LEAD A CAMPAIGN TO VICTORY?

Now that you have inventoried and toured your community, do you have a visceral understanding of the people in your community? Take a hard look at the data and ask yourself, can my cause or candidate succeed?

Now match your visceral understanding with political reality. Do you have the relationships necessary to take the top leadership role in campaigning for a ballot measure or as a candidate for office? Do you have the optimal relationships, experience, and track record in your community to put together the management, message, money, and mobilization that are needed to win?

If you are making a decision as a candidate, be clear about your aptitudes. California progressive strategist Alex Clemens, who runs the SFUsualSuspects.com Web site tracking San Francisco Bay Area politics and policy, offers the following advice to aspiring leaders: "Identify the issues you would take to the barricades. Determine if you are the best person to take the lead for your issue on this campaign: go to your mountaintop, speak to your rabbis [mentors], and be honest with yourself. If this is a fit, go for it. If not, find the person who is the best fit, and support them."[16] In that vein, Dan Maffei, a candidate for Congress in New York in 2006 and 2008, told me that when he decided to run, he was told by a key mentor: "Assume that you are on your own." The lesson for campaigns: even with all the networks and party registration numbers that portend success, in the end you have to take personal responsibility to earn every vote and raise each dollar on your own.

If the numbers add up, it is time to recruit people from your community to your cause and empower them with leadership roles in the campaign. If now is not the time, you may wish to gain public service experience by working with a cause or candidate who shares your vision, ideas, and values.

GET REAL: MAP YOUR POLITICAL GEOGRAPHY

1. Prepare a Community Inventory

The People

- How many people live in your community?
- How old are they? How many are seniors? Families? Kids?
- What is the ethnic breakdown of the district?
- How many are renters and how many homeowners?
- What is the per capita income?
- What are the major schools?
- Who are the ten largest employers in the private, public and nonprofit sectors?

The Geography

- Is the community urban, suburban, rural, or a combination?
- What are the parkland, beaches, and other recreation areas?
- What are the transit routes?
- What are the political districts (Supervisor/Assembly/ Congress/and so forth)?
- What are the population and growth centers?
- What are the historical museums, landmarks, and tourist attractions?

The Traditions

- What are the community traditions: the Big Game, annual neighborhood or ethnic festivals, Fourth of July parades, chamber picnics, beach cleanups, 5k races?
- Who leads the community institutions that participate in these traditions: block club presidents, church deacons, shop stewards, PTA presidents?

The Opinion Leaders

- Who are the opinion leaders: newspaper columnists, philanthropists, labor leaders, corporate leaders, nonprofit directors, civil rights and human rights leaders?
- What are the cultural landmarks, places of worship, and institutions: universities, think tanks, foundations, civic engagement organizations, and business associations?

The Politics

- How many voters are eligible, registered, and voting?
- How have populist people and initiatives performed in the past?

- Are voters likely to support you or your opposition in an upcoming election?

- How do people vote: early, absentee, by mail?

- Is there a deciding voting bloc that can determine the outcome of the election?

- How many votes do you, your candidate, or your cause need to succeed?

- Who are the people elected at the local, county, state, and federal levels?

- What are the various political camps in your community, and who is on which side?

- Will you be forced to choose sides, and which side shares your values?

- Which of these political leaders are likely to get involved in your campaign?

The Technology, Coalition, and Human Networks

- List significant technology, coalition, and human networks in your community.

- List campus networks.

2. Connect with Community Service Leaders

- When was the last time you spoke with any of the community leaders you identified?

- What issues are most on their minds?

- What work on issues have you done in the community?

- What fund-raising or organizational work have you done for these community groups and leaders?

- What work have you done with the online communities in your area?

- What work have you done for (or against) these political leaders?

3. Gut check: do you have a visceral understanding of your people?

- How well do you know the people and traditions in your community inventory?

- How familiar are you with the ideals and ideas of the people?

- Are you the best person to step forward for your cause or candidate?

- Can you garner enough support for your cause or candidate to win?

THREE

Build Your Leadership Teams

Leadership requires "physical stamina and the abilities to
think strategically, to be tactically nimble, to select good staff
· members and use their advice and criticism, and to respond
to surprises and setbacks." —*George F. Will*

George F. Will's observation was made with respect to presidential candidates, but the attributes are essential for leaders at all levels of aspiration who seek to launch effective campaigns for candidates and causes.

Management requires a *campaign staff and volunteer leadership team* to hardwire these leadership attributes—physical stamina, strategic thinking, nimble tactics, good recruitment, and responsiveness to surprises and setbacks—into a winning plan as well as a *kitchen cabinet* of trusted advisers to assist with sensitive decisions. Message requires a team of *house meeting hosts* to bring the campaign into the community. Money requires a *finance council* to raise the funds necessary for success. Mobilization requires a vibrant *volunteer corps*. For a ballot initiative or candidate, mobilization also requires an *election protection team* to be sure that supporters vote and that their votes are counted as cast.

Each of these teams—campaign staff and volunteer leadership, kitchen cabinet, house meeting hosts, finance council,

volunteer corps, and election protection team—must organize people around a shared vision, work with them in a disciplined way, build a culture of service within the campaign,
and help achieve the vision.

In a broader sense, each member of these teams is an ambassador for the larger social movement promoting a public
service mission and the small-business startup needing a
nuts-and-bolts strategy for success.

YOUR VALUES AND ETHICS SET THE TONE OF YOUR PUBLIC SERVICE

Your values and ethics will set the tone of your public service. First and foremost, you have to be yourself. All too often,
people will get into trouble when, rather than being confident in their service mission, they adapt their views to more
experienced people in exchange for what they think will be a
more easily obtained endorsement or contribution. Bad idea.
You have to be you, and you have to convey the same service
mission to everyone.

People may offer contributions for your organization,
cause, or candidate and then tell you they expect a particular
outcome. Stop the conversation. No contribution is worth
your soul, much less your liberty and reputation. Other people
may urge you to use negative information about the opposition, or they will tell you unsavory details of their conversations with other people. A simple rule applies: "If they'll do it
for you, they'll do it to you." Once you ditch your old supporters for new friends, your new friends will know how little
you value friendship and feel free to ditch you on the same
grounds. That is why ethics are so critical to the way you conduct yourself. If you wish to be relieved of your commitment
to others, do not be surprised if they in turn wish to be relieved

of their commitment to you. Think long and hard before you abandon your values, your friends, or your commitments.

When you undertake the leadership of a campaign, you become responsible for anything that goes out to the public. Establish clear ethical standards and expectations for practices such as fund-raising, and clear policies for endorsements, questionnaires, and Internet use.

The first sign of life in a twenty-first-century campaign is usually an e-mail announcing a campaign with a link to a Web site. The person sending that e-mail is the campaign's first ambassador. Therefore, from the start it is essential to establish protocols for every ambassador, beginning with Internet use. Nothing instills more confidence than a welcoming Web site or doubt more quickly than an egregiously inappropriate e-mail.

Welcoming Web site. Your Web site is the first glimpse that many people will have of your campaign. Make sure that it reflects the vision, ideas, and values of your public service mission. It should be welcoming to your visitors and encourage them to volunteer, contribute, and network. Be scrupulous with this personal data: do not share the information with anyone except the appropriate campaign finance reporting entities, and do not sell it to anyone.

Be sure that your information technology vendor understands your ethics. Your site should avoid spyware technology that may violate the privacy of your visitors, and should be constantly updated and checked for viruses. If someone made a personal visit to your home, you wouldn't look through their wallet, sell their personal information, or make them sick. Don't do that when they pay a virtual visit to your campaign Web site.

Egregiously inappropriate e-mail. No medium is more permissive and less forgiving than the Internet. What happens in a flash or on a whim lasts into perpetuity. "Netiquette"— the etiquette of using the Internet—is essential to any twenty-first-century public service effort.

A few basic rules of netiquette:

1. If you wouldn't say it off-line, DON'T say it online.
2. DON'T forward other people's e-mails without their permission.
3. DO assume that other people will forward your e-mail without your permission.
4. DO save copies of important e-mails and posted items for backup and verification.
5. If you get a group e-mail rather than a blind copy, DON'T harvest it for e-mail addresses.
6. If someone calls you on a netiquette lapse, DO apologize in real time and move on.
7. DON'T forget that *www* stands for *World Wide Web*— there is no "private" e-mail!

Ignore these rules of netiquette at your peril. In an infamous example of inappropriate behavior outed by technology, Florida GOP Congressman Mark Foley went into rehab after media publication of his e-mails to a sixteen-year-old former Capitol Hill page.[1] Apart from highly questionable conduct, Foley forgot a fundamental rule of the information superhighway: the *e* in *e-mail* can stand for *evidence*. His district is now represented by Democrat Tim Mahoney.

MANAGEMENT: CAMPAIGN STAFF AND VOLUNTEER LEADERSHIP

Every campaign is a small-business startup with a short time to build and sell a concept to potential supporters and to achieve a winning result.

This venture requires excellent management. Recruit a campaign staff and a volunteer leadership team to hardwire leadership attributes—physical stamina, strategic thinking, nimble tactics, good recruitment, and responsiveness to surprises and setbacks—into a winning plan.

Physical stamina. A winning campaign will require an aggressive schedule to advance your message. AFSCME political director Larry Scanlon often says that campaign leaders should remember: don't ask people to do anything that you are not willing to do yourself. If you are asking people to give up their time, energy, and resources and put their reputations on the line, you have to do the same, and you have to be willing to do whatever it takes in working sixteen-hour days for months at a time. Be sure that you have the commitment to service, family support, and physical stamina for this. Other than a limited amount of time—brief workouts, weekly worship, family celebrations, and holidays—you will have to give over your personal time to the public service campaign.

If you are working on a campaign for public office or running yourself, consider these candidate duties. "Candidates at all levels of political aspiration who are serious about winning spend most of their time fund-raising, attending public events, speaking with the press, and maintaining political relationships with other officials and organizations," advises Jim Gonzalez, chair of the New House PAC, who ran for office four times over a twenty-year period in San Francisco and served as county supervisor and deputy mayor.[2] Candidates also spend a great deal of time going door-to-door and attending house meetings to speak with voters.

Finally, candidates must be aware of all major financial and legal filings, compliance exercises, and related decisions. Candidates must be prepared to delegate the rest to their

CALL TO SERVICE

FRED ROSS

Fred Ross Jr. heard his call to service through the work of his father, Fred Ross Sr., and United Farmworkers of America president Cesar Chavez. Ross recalls: "I grew up in a household where fighting injustice was a way of life, from my father's tireless organizing in the barrios and fields to my mother's, Frances Ross's, pioneering work with the mentally ill." In 1964 Fred Ross Sr. organized Yaqui Indian and Mexican American families in Guadalupe, Arizona, for "the simplest justice: paved streets, traffic lights on a dangerous two-lane highway, and basic services that other communities took for granted," recalls Ross Jr. "One night, after 897 residents had registered to vote, the newly formed Guadalupe Organization, G.O., held its first town meeting. What I saw that night was a classic example of how people organize, build power, and hold elected officials accountable. I saw it in the faces and voices of men and women who had never spoken publicly before [who] got up and peppered the candidates with tough questions. That experience made me immensely proud of my father, seeing how an organizer changes lives and gives people the tools to build power and win justice."

Now a senior strategist with the Service Employees International Union (SEIU), Ross reflects: "I learned from Cesar Chavez and my father that the organizer works quietly behind the scenes, patiently asking questions, listening respectfully, agitating, teaching new leaders, pushing them to take action and create hope *con animo,* 'with great enthusiasm.'"

Source: Excerpted from Fred Ross, foreword to *Cesar Chavez: Autobiography of La Causa,* by Jacques E. Levy (Minneapolis: University of Minnesota Press, 2007), reprinted by permission of the University of Minnesota Press.

campaign staff and volunteer leadership. In the law, it is said that an attorney who represents herself has a fool for a client. In politics, the same can be said for a candidate who wants to manage herself.

If you are working on a cause, you may not have a timetable as concrete as a specific Election Day. That gives you all the more reason to demonstrate stamina as you move through the political process, creating coalitions one person at a time to bring about social change.

"When we began our effort to defeat the Reagan–Oliver North policy of military aid for the Contras in Nicaragua, most people thought it couldn't be done," recalls Fred Ross Jr., who organized the effort with a network called Neighbor to Neighbor. How did Ross and Neighbor to Neighbor beat the odds and change the policies of a popular president? They built moral, economic, and political coalitions one person at a time, took collective action, created controversy, and spoke truth to power in a forceful, imaginative way. "From 1986 to 1988, over 100 Neighbor to Neighbor organizers were deployed to eleven states and eighteen congressional districts— swing voters to cut off Contra aid. We mobilized 70,000 Americans in our national grassroots pressure campaign, combining it with creative media campaigns that reached 20 million people. In 1988, Congress voted by a 219–211 margin against Contra aid, marking the first defeat for Reagan's foreign policy in Central America. Our campaign made the difference."[3]

Strategic thinking. The primary purpose of a campaign staff and volunteer leadership team is to craft a campaign plan that lays out a strategy to win. Jim Gonzalez advises: "A campaign plan must answer who, what, when, where, why, and how you are going to put forward the best message and deliver that message as many times as possible to as many of your targeted supporters as possible."

Let's say that your campaign plan is for a ballot initiative or candidate and your supporters are defined as potential voters on Election Day. These are the elements of strategic thinking that must go into the plan for success:

Who? Your target voters are those people eligible to vote who might vote for you or your cause. Start with the microtargeting work you did to cross-check your voter file with your community inventory data, commercially available consumer information, personal Rolodexes, membership lists, and input from individual volunteers who have reached these voters directly. People who will never vote for someone from your party, who will never support your position on the ballot issue, who never make it to the polls, or who are not legally allowed to vote are not your targets. Who will you target?

What? Your campaign must develop a message that energizes people ready to support you, that wins over some people who do not start in your column, and that divides the people who are planning to oppose you. What will your message be?

When? You should deliver your message to your targeted supporters as many times as possible. When will you start your communications program?

Where? You must reach your targeted supporters where they live and where they get their political information, whether that means knocking on their doors, appearing on their television sets, visiting them online, or texting their cell phones. Where will your campaign contact people?

Why? Winning is the reason for everything you do in a campaign for a ballot initiative or candidate.

What is the "win number" (one vote over 50 percent of the votes cast) to carry your cause or candidate to victory?

How? Given limited resources, you must maximize efficiency. For example, convincing people who vote in every election to vote for your team is generally easier (and therefore less expensive) than convincing people who never vote to start voting and then cast their ballots for you. What will your strategy be?

Bottom line: Do you believe you can put together your win number to support your campaign? Can you capture one vote over 50 percent of the votes that will be cast on Election Day?

Once you have laid out this plan, you can attract investors (supporters) and build a team to implement it. Campaigns should have a summarized campaign plan available on the Web site, in the fund-raising kits, in house meeting packets, and at headquarters. Once there is a plan, people can be recruited into the operational part of the plan that makes sense for their skills and interests.

See, for example, the campaign plan summary given to each volunteer who entered the Nancy Pelosi for Congress headquarters during her special election campaign in 1987.

Nimble tactics. You have to be, in the words of AFSCME's Larry Scanlon, "nimble, creative, and opportunistic" because you can't take the politics out of politics.[4] No matter how well thought-out your plan, political considerations will require you to shift gears quickly. A big donor you were counting on pulls her funding; you better shift gears and find the money someplace else. A newspaper editorial comes out slamming your ballot initiative; you may respond with increased media buys to counter the effect. Suddenly your race

NANCY PELOSI FOR CONGRESS: THE JUNE 2 VICTORY PLAN

I. Goal: Win the June 2nd election by getting 60,000 votes for Nancy Pelosi for Congress

II. Where the Votes Will Come From?
    Because this is a special election, the danger is that most people may forget to vote—only 111,000 voted in the primary.
    We know that there are 30,000 Democrats who always vote—the perennial voters. We can count on them. But to get 60,000 votes, we need 30,000 more—from those Democrats who only occasionally vote. The most effective way to do this is to get them to vote early by mail.
    On Tuesday, April 28, Congresswoman Barbara Boxer and Senator Alan Cranston sent a letter to all Democrats asking them to return an enclosed "Vote by Mail" application. Between now and May 25, we will contact 20,000 of these voters to urge them to vote by mail. Then, between May 25 and June 2, we will remind the remaining 10,000 Democrats to go to the polls on Election Day.

for public office gets more or less crowded; someone jumps in and grabs some of your support, or someone drops out and you have to chase their supporters. Your plan should have some flexibility for these nimble tactics. Assume that the other side is working just as hard as you are to think fast, react forcefully, and seize opportunities.

III. How Will We Do It?

1. The Precinct Leaders, by walking and phoning their neighborhoods, will deliver 30 votes by mail per precinct. With 120 precinct leaders, this equals 3,600 votes for Nancy.

2. The Phone Bank will call five nights a week for three weeks. With 20 phone volunteers delivering 30 votes by mail each night, this equals 9,000 votes for Nancy.

3. The Ironing Board Brigade of 75 volunteers working on the streets will deliver 2,160 votes by mail each weekend for the next four weeks. This equals another 8,640 votes for Nancy.

4. Neighborhood Meetings. Between May 12 and May 23, Nancy will meet with her supporters in 8 neighborhoods to thank them for their support and exchange ideas.

5. GOTV [Get Out the Vote]. Finally, from May 30th to June 2nd, we will call and visit all those Democrats who didn't vote by mail and make sure 10,000 get out to vote on Election Day June 2.

Good recruitment. A winning plan needs a diverse team of people who have demonstrated success in the profession and leadership in the community. It means hiring staff and consultants with skills, experience, and good reputations.

Your campaign staff and volunteer leadership team must include people who know more than you do. Those who

— CAMPAIGN CALENDAR —

MONDAY	TUESDAY	WEDNESDAY	THURSDAY	FRIDAY	SATURDAY	SUNDAY
27	28	29	30	1 — M·A·Y	2 — KICK-OFF RALLY — PHASE I	3 — 1 IRONING BOARD BRIGADE
4 — A·P·R·I·L	5	6 — PRECINCT LEADERS GET 3600 VOTES: BY MAIL / IRONING BOARD BRIGADE GETS 3600 VOTES: BY MAIL / PHONE BANK GETS 9000 VOTES: BY MAIL	7	8 — PLANNING SESSION FOR NEIGHBORHOOD MEETINGS	9 — 1 IRONING BOARD BRIGADE	10 — 1 IRONING BOARD BRIGADE
11	12	13	14 — PLANNING SESSION FOR NEIGHBORHOOD MEETINGS	15	16 — 1 IRONING BOARD BRIGADE	17 — 1 IRONING BOARD BRIGADE
18	19	20	21	22	23 — 1 IRONING BOARD BRIGADE	24 — 1 IRONING BOARD BRIGADE
25 — LAST DAY TO TURN IN VOTE BY MAIL APP!	26 — PHASE II ★	27	28 — G	29 — O	30 — T	31 — V
1 — J·U·N·E — ELECTION DAY! ★						

think they know it all and surround themselves with people who reinforce that perception are doomed to fail. A confident leader draws upon the best resources available and is not afraid to learn from experts.

As national communications strategist Jamal Simmons advises, "People will tell you the truth—either to your face or behind your back. It's up to you to create an environment where they can tell you to your face." For instance, when Simmons worked for Mickey Kantor, commerce secretary in the Clinton-Gore administration, he was told "don't blow smoke" by his boss, who wanted an honest critique of his performance after speeches and interviews.[5]

Choose people who can work together as a team for long hours under intense pressure. Everyone will be an advocate for their part of the campaign: message people will want polls and media ads; mobilization people will want field program dollars. Choose people who can debate internally and then leave internal discussions behind to emerge as "one team, one fight."

Ultimately it is the campaign leader or candidate who will have to assess all the needs and make a decision. As Dotty LeMieux cautions: "Know that you can't please everyone. The old adage, 'Too many cooks spoil the broth' is true in politics as in cooking. Of course you want to get input from others, but some candidates just can't seem to say 'no.' They forget there's a chain of command, and want to take everyone's advice. They're nervous and insecure and it shows. You hired a consultant and staff to advise you based on their experience in doing campaigns. You can't be all things to all people."[6]

Responsiveness to surprises and setbacks. Every public service effort has its bad days. One of those unwelcome surprises turns

CAMPAIGN JOBS AND JOB DESCRIPTIONS

Campaign Manager: Runs day-to-day operation of the campaign. Has final approval on the campaign plan and is responsible for keeping the campaign on track with its goals and for making sure campaign decisions are made efficiently.

Scheduler: Creates opportunities to get the message out and keeps the campaign calendar.

Fund-Raising Director: Works with finance council to identify new sources of potential contributions and strives to bring that money into the campaign.

Communications Director: Directs paid and free media operations.

Internet Coordinator: Operates and updates blog; facilitates direct communication with volunteers, netroots communities, and online communities; expands Internet presence to technol-

up in the news one day, and the campaign morale plummets. It may not even be a crisis but a disappointment: you work your heart out for an endorsement, and it goes to the other side. You raise less money than you thought; you get a bad poll; your allies have other priorities. If you believe in what you are doing, you will have the strength to fall and get back up numerous times. Successful campaigns remain optimistic and true to their service mission, and they address problems up front.

ogy, coalition, and human networks; and provides real-time feedback.

Field Director: Mobilizes volunteers to bring out voters; organizes house meeting hosts and get-out-the-vote efforts.

Legal Counsel: Handles such issues as petitions, financial disclosures, and Election Day activities; coordinates election protection team.

Treasurer: Balances the books, issues checks, files campaign disclosure reports.

Research Director: Directs research on people and issues.

Database Manager: Keeps computerized voter file, volunteer lists, and fund-raising lists current.

Volunteer Coordinator: Recruits, schedules, and supervises volunteers. Builds leadership teams of volunteers through repeated expressions of appreciation of their call to service, skills sets, and feedback.

If you have bad news, take it directly to the leadership team. "Don't spin the bad news," cautions Lezlee Westine. Reflecting on her experience as a senior adviser to President George W. Bush, Westine recommends giving the news "first, fast, straightforward, simple, and solution-oriented."[7] First, because it's better to get bad news from allies rather than be blindsided. Fast, straightforward, and simple, with "no sugar coating," so people know what they are up against.

Solution-oriented, to help your team figure out how to fix the problem. People are relying on you to exercise candor and judgment, so be up front about what's wrong and what can be done to make it right.

If you have a more serious crisis brewing, it's time to bring in the kitchen cabinet.

MANAGEMENT: KITCHEN CABINET

A kitchen cabinet is a management team of trusted friends, colleagues, and family members who know how you receive advice and criticism and can speak truth to power when necessary. They know your character—your core values, code of ethics, and call to service. They provide advice and counsel to campaign leaders on a volunteer basis and assist with rapid response in the wake of surprises or setbacks.

In building your kitchen cabinet, consider:

Advice and criticism. How do you receive advice and criticism? Who are the people you already engage in that process? Whom do you trust to give you constructive criticism? If you make a mistake, whose advice should you take?

Friends. In public life, there are "first-name friends" and "last-name friends." First-name friends are people who know and appreciate you for you: they know you outside of politics, and their personal ambition does not depend on your professional success. Last-name friends know and appreciate you for your public persona or agenda and can be great allies, but they are not necessarily trusted advisers. It's great to have both first-name friends and last-name friends—you just have to know who is who, and whom you can trust. Add first-name friends who know your core to your kitchen cabinet.

Build your kitchen cabinet with the following advisers:

1. Family members who can give you good personal advice.

2. Political or civic mentors with experience and judgment in managing public service campaigns and in responding swiftly to surprises and setbacks.

3. First-name friends who know and appreciate you outside of public life and who can advise you because their ambition does not depend on your professional success.

4. An ally from the opposite side of the aisle who can provide a reality check because their philosophy does not depend on the success of your campaign.

If you are a member of someone's kitchen cabinet or senior staff, your responsibility is to report bad news and provide helpful alternatives while maintaining the privacy and integrity of the person you are advising.

Those who know don't talk, and those who talk don't know. The ideal is a kitchen cabinet whose members provide unvarnished feedback and bad news along with constructive solutions with a minimum of gossip and a maximum of discretion. As with any other internal deliberation, advice should be offered behind the scenes, not in the newspapers. Advice should be discreet and direct—a discreet conversation with a direct approach to the issues at hand.

If you are facing a crisis, get out in front of it: set forth your version of events, provide supporting documentation if applicable, communicate with your supporters and the public, and then get back on track.

Rapid response is particularly important in the modern era of the twenty-four-hour image cycle. The arc of a scandal is generally the same: *recognition* of the issue with candor and contrition as appropriate, acceptance of personal *respon-*

sibility for any mistakes, *recommitment* to service, and *redemption* through trustworthy behavior. People tend to want to move on and focus on their future, and they will be more likely to do so if they can trust their public servants to do so as well. Any delay in this narrative—or relapse—will be politically perilous.

Thus, waiting days to respond to charges only makes them seem more credible or leads people to question your answers when they do come. The old adage about Watergate—"The cover-up was worse than the crime"—is how we measure modern crisis management. The situation morphs from an individual criticism or mistake into an overall impression that a candidate does not have the strength of character to listen to the counsel of wise people, or that he has something even worse in his background. Get it all out there (recognition), own up to it (responsibility), get back to your service mission (recommitment), and rebuild people's trust (redemption).

MESSAGE: HOUSE MEETING HOSTS

Why house meetings? You need a strategy that brings your message into the community, allows you to meet your neighbors, and attracts volunteers to your campaign. There is no better message preparation or refinement exercise than speaking in the living rooms of your constituents. Whether they are friends, volunteers, elected officials, or community activists, your house meeting hosts are people who have agreed to open their homes to neighbors who are invited to come "kick the tires" on a the candidacy.

Once you come together in the early stages of a campaign, house meeting hosts are full partners in your campaign—

and in your career. In spring 1987, Fred Ross Jr. ran the field program for the Nancy Pelosi for Congress special election campaign, using the house meeting model to connect with voters and recruit volunteers. Over 120 house meetings were held in six weeks. Nineteen years later, over a dozen of those house meeting hosts signed her nomination papers for re-election, and dozens more are involved in her ongoing community events.

House meetings are excellent organizing tools for screening films that promote social change and political campaigns as well. Want to attract volunteers to your campaign? Make DVDs and organizational materials available for people to screen and discuss. Whether for a candidate or a cause, the film must include personal stories and testimonials that draw people to the effort.

House meetings are therefore not just coffee klatches or quick stops on the candidate's schedule; they are your opportunity to grow your grassroots army and connect with people for the long term. They don't take more than an hour, but they require focus, respect, preparation, and follow-up to be sure that your message is heard in homes throughout the community.

MONEY: FINANCE COUNCIL

A public service campaign finance council consists of a finance chair, a treasurer, a fund-raising director, and key donors. The finance chair is a well-respected member of the community who has a track record in support of your public service mission. This person will lead the fund-raising effort. The treasurer balances the books, issues checks, and files campaign disclosure reports. The fund-raising director works with the finance council to identify new sources of potential contributions and to bring that money into the campaign. This work begins with donors who may already be part of your informal finance council, people such as those with whom you have raised funds for other causes and candidates.

This team is responsible for implementing the campaign finance plan by attracting the support of their friends and colleagues. As a preliminary matter, the finance council creates the campaign budget.

A public service campaign budget is the campaign plan expressed in dollars and cents over time. As with the campaign plan, your budget should express a clear strategy to capture 50 percent of the votes cast plus one additional vote to win the election. It should cover the staff and materials required by each of the four major parts of your campaign: message, management, mobilization, and money.

The real work of a campaign is communicating with voters. Campaigns can generally be rated according to how much money actually goes into the communications budget. The following percentages are meant to provide you with a rough guideline to creating a strong budget: management: 5 percent; message/media: 65 percent; money: 10 percent; mobilization: 20 percent.

Remember that your budget must accurately reflect the various time intervals of a campaign. Do you qualify for matching funds at a certain point? Is there a large fund-raiser scheduled for July 4? These are the types of issues that you will face in creating a working campaign budget. Once you have created your budget, it is the job of the campaign manager to stick to it. For this reason, many campaigns have a rule that only the campaign manager can authorize expenditures. Even the candidate is not allowed to spend—or promise to spend— money without getting approval first from the manager.

It is ultimately the job of the campaign manager to make sure there is still enough money in the budget at the end of the campaign to cover all expenses. The campaign manager must also make sure that the campaign does not end with a loss at the polls and a lot of money left in the bank. The goal of a good campaign is to spend exactly what is needed—and not a penny more—to win.

If you are working with a nonprofit, your finance council performs as the quality-control team. It may be a subset of your board of directors and include your auditing and accounting staff. Be sure to check your expenses and maintain exquisite records. TechNet's Lezlee Westine says that as CEO of a $3 million nonprofit, she checks her budget every week. That kind of scrupulous vigilance can help keep track of your finances and keep faith with your investors and the public.

MOBILIZATION: VOLUNTEER CORPS

A vibrant volunteer corps is the heart and soul of a public service campaign. The volunteer corps is generally led by the volunteer coordinator and includes trusted volunteers who believe in the campaign and have invested time training new people as they come in to the effort.

If you are a potential volunteer, evaluate the public service mission of a campaign. Ask to see a copy of the campaign plan so you can determine what activities are going on and what appeals to you. You may find that once you try something new—like phone-banking—you will want to do more of it, or you may find that there is something else that you like better.

Volunteers and campaigns should be flexible and willing to try out different needs and make the match. Specific volunteer activities are set forth in chapter 7, Mobilize to Win, but for the purposes of building your leadership teams, you should devote resources to volunteer coordinators who can give each potential volunteer a brief welcome interview, lay out the plan, experiment with different activities to find a match, and be enthusiastic, patient, and thankful.

This way of mobilizing builds a culture of service within the campaign, where each person's contribution—to any of the leadership teams or organizational needs—is a force multiplier.

MOBILIZATION: ELECTION PROTECTION TEAM

An election protection team develops the strategy to ensure that supporters vote and that their votes are counted as cast. If you are working on a campaign for elected office, you must know how the votes are being cast and counted. On a political campaign, the temptation will be to save get-out-the-vote efforts for the last days before Election Day. Big mistake. You need to begin at the inception of your campaign.

Just as your code of ethics sets the tone of your campaign, your commitment to justice sets the tone of your election protection team. Election protection efforts reflect your vision to advance civil rights, promote voting rights, and conduct oversight of voting systems. From voter registration to recount, you must have a council of voting experts and lawyers, including members of constituency groups who have voting rights expertise, keeping an eye on your votes at all times.

Voting rights advocate Donna Brazile describes voting as "one of our most sacred and important rituals" and cautions that voting is "still threatened every election day by uninformed poll workers, technology, campaigns more interested in winning than an individual's right, and election laws that don't always make sense."[8]

DONNA BRAZILE

Ultimately the power in our democracy derives from the people, not a king or politician, and it is best exercised by having the fullest public participation in elections and service. Donna Brazile, who has spent a lifetime in politics offering her expertise as an author, pundit, and Gore for president campaign manager in 2000, traces her interest in voting rights to her youth:

As a child growing up in the Deep South during the civil rights revolution, I wanted to get involved and help create the change that I was witnessing every day. On the night Dr. Martin Luther King Jr. was assassinated, I made a personal vow to God to work for change and to help make a difference. Soon I found myself working alongside other civil rights workers to register people to vote and helping out during election season. I was riveted by the passion of those civil rights workers who were both courageous and determined to have a seat at the table where public policy decisions were being made. They were my inspiration. Their sacrifice and commitment to the ideals of freedom and equality gave me hope for the future and led me to dedicate my own life to helping to keep the dream of justice and equality for all—regardless of race, gender, class, disability, age, or sexual orientation. We are all God's children, and no one deserves to be treated as a second-class citizen.

Source: Donna Brazile, e-mail, June 4, 2007.

Your election protection team should include voting experts and lawyers. More details will follow in chapter 7, Mobilize to Win, but for team-building purposes, you will want to start with people such as local county election officials who know the people who have custody of the voter file. Add people who understand the voting patterns of the community, including representatives of constituency groups who have voting rights expertise and who can add counsel and help with get-out-the-vote efforts across the electorate. Particular areas of concern are hot spots such as early voting, military ballots, and student voting that tend to raise voting rights issues.

After all the hard work of your leadership teams to develop and implement the campaign plan, you will want to make sure that your public service campaign ends in victory, with every supporter voting and every vote counted as cast.

GET REAL: BUILD YOUR LEADERSHIP TEAMS

Campaigns are often shaped by character and events. Campaign teams made up of people who know your character can best help you create and respond to events in a manner that will effectively promote your message. Develop a strategy to build your teams:

1. Management: Campaign Staff and Volunteer Leadership

- Who can I attract to my diverse team of people with skills, experience and good reputations who can work together as "one team, one fight"?
- Who has won elections and built coalitions in this community?
- Who are effective ambassadors for my cause?

2. Management: Kitchen Cabinet

- How do I best receive advice and feedback?
- If I make a mistake, whose advice should I take?
- What family members give me good personal advice?
- Who are my political or civic mentors with experience and judgment in managing public service campaigns and in responding swiftly to surprises and setbacks?
- Who are my first-name friends who know and appreciate me outside of public life and who can advise me because their ambition does not depend on my professional success?
- Who is an ally from the opposite side of the aisle who can provide a reality check because their philosophy does not depend on the success of my campaign?

3. Message: House Meeting Hosts

- Looking at my networks, whom can I ask to be my first set of house meeting hosts?
- Who among my friends, family, work colleagues, and nonprofit allies will sign up?
- Who has a history of hosting house meetings for causes similar to my campaign?

4. Money: Finance Council

- Who serves as my finance chair, treasurer, and fundraising director?
- Who is already in my informal finance council? With whom have I raised funds for other causes and candidates?
- Whom should I include to attract support from donors, netroots communities, and grassroots communities, and what is my strategy to reach them?

5. Mobilization: Volunteer Corps

- Who are the key volunteers I can target from networks in my community inventory?
- Who are trusted supporters who can organizers others with enthusiasm and appreciation?

6. Mobilization: Election Protection Team

- Who knows who has custody of the voter file? Who knows the voting patterns of the community?
- Which members of constituency groups who have voting rights expertise can add counsel to my campaign?
- Who can help me with get-out-the-vote efforts in hot spots such as early voting, military ballots, and student voters?

FOUR

Define Your Message

What we've got here is a failure to communicate.
—Cool Hand Luke

Match the person to the adjective:

Ronald Reagan	resolved
George H. W. Bush	optimistic
Bill Clinton	stiff
Al Gore	empathetic
George W. Bush	reserved

Like the political leaders listed above, you may ultimately be defined by just one word. Your challenge is to pick that word before anyone else does. If you end up with the wrong word, you have a failure to communicate.

You must lead with who you are. If you are working with a candidate for office, what do you want your volunteers to say when someone encounters them in an elevator and asks, "Why are you wearing a button for her?" If you run a non-profit and someone sees your organization's slogan, what would you tell them it means? You need a clear, concise argument promoting your effort, something the other person will take home and think about later. This description, also known as an "elevator pitch," is the heart of your message.

FRAME YOUR MESSAGE WITH A MESSAGE BOX

Defining your message means articulating your vision, ideas, and values. Refining your message means finding ways to persuade people to choose your vision, ideas, and values over those of your competition. People do not make choices in a vacuum: for every good reason you can think of for people to embrace your message, there may well be a counterpoint. In order to present your strongest case, you must identify the counterpoint and rebut it. As Jack Valenti often advised, to be a credible messenger, you must be up front about your weaknesses and your opponents' strengths.

A helpful exercise in laying out campaign messages is the message-box exercise. Democratic lore has it that the message box was popularized by Paul Tully, a national strategist who trained legions of campaign workers with this exercise during the 1980s.

Here's how it works: you draw a simple four-square box to summarize your message with what you say about yourself, what your opponent says about herself, and what both sides say about the other.

What You Say About You—put your best case forward.

What They Say About Them—put their best case forward.

What You Say About Them—why are you better and/or why are they worse?

What They Say About You—what is their best case against you and/or why are they better than you?

What You Say About You	What They Say About Them
What You Say About Them	What They Say About You

A message box frames what's at stake in the debate, clarifies what you say, and helps you play defense. You will see where your opponent will attack you, how you can respond, and how you can move the conversation back to your message.

You must present a clear choice and a definite contrast with your opposition (be it opposition to a person or an issue). A message box helps articulate that choice and keeps your campaign disciplined. Every strategic messaging decision you make should be consistent with your message box.

YOUR MESSAGE BEGINS
WITH YOUR CALL TO SERVICE

What You Say About You should express your call to service. Whether you are a candidate for office, a volunteer for a campaign or a policy advocate, your personal story builds trust between you and your audience. Your call to service—your vision, ideas, and values—demonstrates why you care about people and why people should care about you.

Three recent candidates expressed their public service aspirations as part of their campaign messages:

Retired Admiral Joe Sestak was elected to Congress with a message about health care. "I learned about health care in

America from the other side of the curtain," said Sestak. Sestak's young daughter had a brain tumor, and thanks to his U.S. Navy benefits, she received excellent care. His daughter's hospital roommate on the other side of the curtain had to struggle to piece together enough insurance coverage to stay. "We were lucky—I have veterans health care because of you; I am running to be sure every child in America has health care. I am going make my service about exactly that."[1]

Congresswoman Kirsten Gillibrand of New York was raised in the tradition of public service: as a child, she campaigned with her grandmother, who founded Albany's first women's Democratic club and was a pioneer in the women's rights movement. "As a ten-year-old girl, I would listen to my grandmother discuss issues, and she made a lasting impression on me," Gillibrand said. She credits her success to her grandmother's mentoring, which inspired her to participate in a range of public service networks promoting women, social justice, and the environment.[2]

Congressman Jerry McNerney of California was inspired to run by his son Michael, who in response to the 9/11 attacks sought and received a commission in the U.S. Air Force. Michael suggested that Jerry serve his country by running for the U.S. Congress, and McNerney accepted the challenge. He lost in 2004 but prevailed in 2006. One of McNerney's mailers depicted a young servicemember on the cover asking, "How do I know that Jerry McNerney will protect veterans?" The response: "Because he's my Dad." This message vividly displayed McNerney's call for peace and veterans' rights contrasted with his pro-war incumbent opponent who voted to raise his own congressional pay while refusing to raise combat pay and veterans disability benefits.[3]

Each of the messages—by Sestak, Gillibrand, and

McNerney—expresses the call to service (health care, good government, veterans' rights) and points to the family member (daughter, grandmother, son) who helped inspire the call.

What You Say About You should inspire trust. Each aspiring public servant must show that they can be trusted to serve people, to do something and not just be something. "It boils down to trust," says communications strategist Jamal Simmons. "At the end of the day when you are alone in that room and nobody can see, the public must believe that you will look out for them."[4]

How will people come to trust you? Because you have taken a political risk, taken the lead on an issue, sacrificed for a cause. You will have a track record: your voter registration, your votes, your volunteer work, your charitable contributions, your advocacy for others, your performance in appointed or elected office. Your track record reinforces your message.

To perform this exercise yourself, start at the very beginning. Let's say your campaign is for a challenger with no government experience and the opponent's team is supporting an entrenched incumbent. Your message begins with Youth versus Experience.

What You Say About You	*What They Say About Them*
Youth is a fresh face.	Experience will get things done.
What You Say About Them	*What They Say About You*
Experience is the system, and the system is broken.	Youth lacks the experience to get anything done.

CULTIVATE EXPERTS AND ALLIES TO HELP DELIVER YOUR MESSAGE

"Message is so much more than what you say. People will look at who says it, who corroborates it, what you are doing when you deliver the message, where you are when you deliver the message, and whether you refresh, reinforce, and repeat your message," says California political strategist Mary Hughes. "How you deliver your message conveys whether your leadership is authentic, attached to the community, and reflective of the people." She recommends cultivating experts and allies to help craft and validate your message.[5]

What You Say About You should address key policy challenges. For example, let's say that part of *What You Say About You* is that you support veterans and military families. You must be aware of key policy challenges and integrate them into your message. You will need to communicate the vision, ideas, and values that will help make tangible change in these areas. To corroborate your message, you need experts and allies. Convene an advisory group featuring all branches of military service and generations of veterans to develop your platform on these issues. Build off your community inventory from chapter 2, Know Your Community, and look into prominent veterans in your community, veterans' service organizations, military bases, and veterans' hospitals. Your advisory group should help you discuss the major challenges: the status of combat operations in Iraq and Afghanistan; rebuilding military readiness after years of war; the cost of war, particularly with respect to lifelong disabilities caused by combat; military recruiting on campuses; the travesty of poor care at Walter Reed and other veterans' hospitals; National Guard employment discrimination; the increasing abuse, divorce, and alcoholism rates among military families; and the challenges faced by veterans returning to the job market after war.

Once you put the message together, develop a calendar of important dates, starting with Memorial Day and Veterans Day, and get your message out to these groups with reinforcement by members of your advisory group. That way, when you say that you will support veterans' rights, you can speak with authority, with the corroboration of experts and allies. When you hold events, repeat your message in your follow-up thank-yous to participants and press releases to the public.

ESTABLISH A POLICY STRATEGY

Your message is not just what you say in speeches or meetings. If you are a candidate, you will be asked to fill out pledges and questionnaires on nearly every topic you can think of. Before you comply, develop a campaign protocol, because each of your answers will shape the rest of the campaign in ways you may not even consider. Candidates for president today are being asked about questionnaires they or their staffs marked off twenty years ago.

Before you sign your name to anything, think about what you want to say in your campaign and whether you want your views expressed by indicating your agreement with pledges written by other people. If you want to make a "no pledge" pledge, which is to say that you want to put your message out and not sign on to other people's agendas, say so at the beginning of the campaign. You may take some heat, but you may take more when your answer to a questionnaire gets posted on the Internet and you spend days explaining that the question wasn't really fair but you agreed more with "yes" than "no" so you marked "yes," and so forth.

If you decide to fill out questionnaires, do not delegate

this task to anyone. Your message should give people a clear and candid expression of your views so that they know where you stand.

RESEARCH TO DEVELOP YOUR MESSAGE

Research *What You Say About You* and *What They Say About Them.* Knowing yourself and your opposition is essential. Research assists with message development, helping to define you and control the campaign dynamic; with polling, by revealing an early assessment of the public's values and priorities; with press, for information and background materials; and with rapid response, when you need quick access to the facts. As you draw your message box, you will want to consider everything publicly available about your opponents and about you.

Ethics are important to your research work. Conduct your research honestly, and report honestly about your findings. Many people have a negative opinion of opposition research, and you do not want your research tactics to become an issue that distracts people from your message.

Make sure your research is fully documented and frequently updated. You should regularly check newspapers, the Internet, and television news coverage. You may be called upon to use your research at any moment. Solid preparation will make these times much easier.

Internet research is critical. Online services are excellent tools that will make your job easier. Many charge a yearly fee; some of these include LexisNexis, Dialog, and U.S. Politics Today. It is important that you know how easy it is to glean information from the Internet about yourself so you can prepare for ensuing questions and attacks. An easy search of your first and last name can turn up thousands of Internet hits with newspaper articles about you, minutes of meetings you have attended, donations you have made, organizations you are in, blog commentaries, family histories, and more. Narrow a search to keywords linked to your first and last name. Keywords can include your place of residence, your business, your spouse's name, or even *scandal, bad, corrupt* (you may be surprised what people have said about you). Paid searches go further, covering national and local publications as well as public records, which can reveal current and previous addresses, your voting record, and any history of liens, bankruptcies, deed transfers, tax records, and mortgage records.

Sometimes the money is the message. You should research campaign contributions to see if certain interests are funding the opposition. If they are, that can become part of your message. "Follow the money," says Dotty LeMieux. "This is the number one rule of politics, and it's fair game for a comparison piece," she says. Sometimes the money is the message, as when a special interest is asserting itself. For example, says LeMieux, a California initiative for a new pipeline sounded like a good idea until the list of contributors appeared. Big development wanted that pipeline for a reason, and it was easily defeated, despite big spending on the other side. "Sometimes the money trail is hard to follow, but it can be your ace in the hole. Sometimes, all you need to do is list the sources of funding for both you and the competition. Tell the voters: 'You be the judge.'" she advises.[6]

EXPRESS VALUES AND ISSUES

Sierra Club executive director Carl Pope advises campaigns to establish a "values bond" with people. "If a candidate talks

RESEARCH CHECKLIST
FOR CANDIDATES

✓ **Voting Record:** Pay special attention to any of your opponent's votes that were controversial. Then look for votes where no one else voted with your opponent or votes where he or she was joined by just a tiny handful of other legislators. These votes may indicate an extreme position on an issue.

✓ **Legislative Activity:** Make sure you know what committees your opponent sits on and what legislation he or she has introduced. Talk to friendly lobbyists or members of your own party to find out about a controversial bill or amendment your opponent may have introduced or supported.

✓ **Legislative Inactivity:** Does your opponent show up for work? How many votes has he or she missed, and were any of these votes on major issues?

✓ **Sources of Income:** Try to identify where your opponent gets his or her money. Be on the lookout for conflicts of interest and other schemes. Does you opponent earn an outside income despite holding what is supposed to be a full-time government job? Does he or she own any property that does not look quite up to code? Has your opponent ever been fired? Are there any corporate boards your opponent sits on, and if so how do those organizations treat their workers?

✓ **Contributor Information:** Who are the major contributors to your opposition, and why do they give? Is there any evidence their contributions influence the decisions your opponent makes in office?

✓ **Press Coverage:** Check both the major newspapers and the local papers to see what your opponent has said in public. Maybe he or she has changed positions on key issues or has gotten

caught up in a scandal. Local newspapers are an especially good source for this type of information. Many politicians are less careful when talking to these types of reporters.

✓ **Press Coverage of Family, Friends, Business Associates, Investments, and the Like:** It is rare to use this sort of information, but it is good to have just in case. It helps you understand people around your opponent and help you predict his or her movements.

✓ **Assets:** Check for property owned by your opponent. Make sure all taxes have been paid. Get the names of business associates.

✓ **Criminal Actions:** Has your opponent, or business associates or others related to him or her, ever been charged with a crime? This information is readily available at most county courthouses. However, you may need to check in several counties where your opponent has lived or worked.

✓ **Civil Actions:** Has anyone filed suit against your opponent or against friends, family, or business associates? What was the outcome?

✓ **Driving Record:** Make sure your opponent has never been arrested for drunk driving or another road offense. Again, you may choose not to use this information, but it is always better to know.

✓ **Official Biography:** Obtain a copy of your opponent's biography and double-check every fact it contains. Candidates have lost elections by lying about their educational background, so investigate everything. It may also be worth noting what your opponent's biography does not contain. Are there large gaps in time?

✓ **Level of detail:** Check out the federal government's Office of Personnel Management Standard Form 85P: Questionnaire for Public Trust Positions to get a feel for the detailed information asked of aspiring presidential appointees.

about values in a way that overlaps with our issues, our people will get excited. "Ban dirty coal" is a position; "promote clean coal" is a values-based agenda. The first one tells people what you are going to do; the second gives us something to do together—it is a values-based agenda that helps build bridges between people."[7]

Campaigns also need to establish "issues bonds" with people. Pope saw polling in which people identified themselves as environment-first voters, meaning that their top priority was the environment—and a large percentage of those environment-first voters said they were staying home. Why would someone stay home if they know the issues? "The church of politics had disappointed them," reflects Pope. "They needed hope before they would vote." With an environmental initiative on the ballot, the Sierra Club needed to establish an issues bond with the environment-first voters, then convince them that the way to promote the issue was to vote. "We had to convince them that their vote would matter and that their vote would be counted. So the phone-bankers told them three things: one, this policy will make it the law to do the right thing for the environment; two, we will be at the polls making sure your vote is counted; and, three, don't you want to try to make a difference one more time?" Many of them turned out, and the initiative passed.[8]

This message strategy was successful and can be applied to any campaign. Establish a values bond and an issues bond before you introduce them to your political cause or candidate. If your candidate supports cleaning up a polluted river, you could tell environment-first voters that your candidate will prevent people from dumping waste in the river. They've heard that before.

Or you could talk to voters about your candidate's vision

CARL POPE

Carl Pope's service to protect the environment began over thirty years ago after he performed civil rights work with the Student Nonviolent Coordinating Committee in Arkansas and family planning work with the Peace Corps in India. "Coming home in 1969," recalls Pope, "I thought of myself as a progressive, not necessarily as an environmentalist. But I came to see that protecting the environment is about what people have in common. Everyone 'owns' the Hudson River, the San Francisco Bay, and Yellowstone. The potential power was organizing for the common good. In 1970 that was true nationally. Now in 2007 this is true globally: if you drive an SUV today, that may affect a monsoon in ten years. We as a species are not programmed to cope with that."

As the Sierra Club's executive director since 1992, Pope sees part of his service as getting people to work together from across the political and economic spectrums to address these challenges. "Politicians need to ask: 'How can we talk about your values and issues in a way that helps you work with other people?' Issue movements like ours spend a lot of time thinking about ways to use our information to build bridges and promote the common good."

Source: Carl Pope, interview, March 27, 2007.

for a clean river and about your candidate's alliance with a clean-water group that is making clean rivers a priority. Now they have a values bond (a shared agenda to clean the river) an issues bond (a shared ally who is actually working to get things done for people), and a much better introduction.

CHOOSE YOUR WORDS CAREFULLY

What You Say About You is heard in the context of a larger message environment. Prepare yourself for how your audience will receive your message, and frame your message accordingly.

Bear in mind the work of two experts in the use of language in American politics: Frank Luntz and George Lakoff. During the 1990s Luntz rose to prominence as he helped change the way conservative politicians used words to describe policies. Luntz's Web site trumpets this work, identifying Luntz's changes in the public vocabulary: transforming the "estate tax" into the "death tax," "school vouchers" into "opportunity scholarships," and "drilling for oil" into "exploring for energy." Luntz's work demonstrates that powerful words can have a powerful impact.[9] Of course the words must be spoken in a message context. Luntz's messaging is built on a generation of efforts by conservative think tanks to convey information to the public by using certain message frames and by training the next generation of conservatives to use them. Just saying "death tax" without a generation of work on an antitax message would have yielded a slogan but no context.

George Lakoff, author of *Don't Think of an Elephant* (2004) and *Thinking Points: Communicating Our American Values and Vision* (2006), applies a linguist's expertise to politics, urging progressive narratives based on values, ideas, issues, and frames. "First, tell people what you stand for. Tell stories that only make sense relative to your values. For example, I might say that I care about people and want to act responsibly on that care. Government is about protection (our health and safety) and empowerment (our courts and infrastructure)." Prepare yourself for how your audience will receive your message and frame your message accordingly.[10]

Luntz and Lakoff impart similar lessons but from different philosophical perspectives: the use of particular words can dictate whether people hear your message in the way in which you intend. You won't know until you look behind the words to the values of the people and the context in which those values have been expressed.

Choosing your words carefully means incorporating input from your experts and allies. It also means applying common sense. Returning to our Youth versus Experience campaign example, let's say that Youth cultivated experts and allies among other young people, which was great. Then Youth decided to hit hard on the age difference between the two candidates. Not careful, not smart. See the effects on the message debate.

What You Say About You	*What They Say About Them*
Youth can bring new people into the process and is not wedded to old ways.	Experience has a track record.
What You Say About Them	*What They Say About You*
Experience is too old for the job.	Youth attacks old people and will never get anything done.

This exchange happened in a recent campaign: a youthful male contender cultivated young allies in his race against an older female incumbent. He said that his alliances could help him get things done for people. He said his opponent could not get things done because she was out of step with the people (fair enough) and because she was too old for the job (big mistake). He did attract new people—to *her* side. At the time, one of her supporters, a woman in her sixties, told me that the challenger was about to find out just how much power so-called old women have to get things done. He did.

A message-box exercise would have shown the young candidate that he needed a more diplomatic way to promote his youth. Instead, he alienated blocs of voters, motivated them to work against him, and undercut his own message that his youth would attract new people to get things done.

USE POLLING TO REFINE YOUR MESSAGE

A winning campaign will spend most of its money to communicate with voters. Polling can tell you what is on voters' minds and how they will hear your message. Without polling, your campaign could spend hundreds of thousands of dollars telling voters something they do not care about or, worse, something with which they disagree. For example, if you are asserting leadership on a local growth initiative, you will want to poll the voters in order to determine whether families in the area want new development; whether they want to use taxpayer dollars to fund it; and whether they are willing to give up parkland or wetlands to accommodate new homes, better roads, or additional schools.

Media coverage of political polls will usually go something like this: "Polls show Bill Clinton at 50 percent and Bob Dole at 38 percent, with 10 percent of the voters undecided. The margin of error for the poll is plus or minus 4 percent." These results are called the "horse race numbers," because they simply report who was leading at the moment the poll was conducted.

Good polls capture much more about a race than who is ahead and who is behind. Polls can help you determine what issues voters believe are most important in an election, which voters are most likely to come out and vote, what percentage of voters are locked into supporting one candidate or the other, what the trends are among the voters and candidates, who has momentum, whether blocs of voters will move depending on a particular issue, what responses are needed to attacks, and whether voters are inclined to believe your response to an attack.

Candidates or ballot initiative spokespersons who have faults that could prove fatal should do a poll before even launching the campaign. There is no reason to go through the effort of a campaign if polls show that huge percentages of people in your community will not vote for someone with your public identity or past history. Similarly, if you are promoting a bond measure, you will want to explore people's attitudes regarding the government's budget deficits and credit rating before you ask them to incur more debt.

An early poll is a benchmark that can provide a snapshot of your starting point: how well the voters know you or your cause and what their mood is toward politics and life in general. Later surveys are tracking polls to find out how your campaign message is being heard.

Low recognition can make polling more complicated for

first-time candidates and policy initiatives that are just emerging on the scene. However, such early polls can still be useful in determining the overall climate of a community and in uncovering the values and issues important to voters. Good poll results can propel more support for your campaign.

Most pollsters charge according to the number of questions contained in their poll. The more questions they ask voters, the longer their phone workers have to stay on the line and the more expensive the poll is to conduct.

Think about the way you will release your information. Some reporters may want to see the whole poll—not just the good news—before they report on any of it. There may also be laws that require that if a campaign releases part of a poll, the entire poll must be made public. A major catastrophe would result for any campaign if it put out positive elements of a poll only to have to disclose the negatives about the candidate, the issue, or the campaign's spokespersons.

Finally, make sure your polling reaches people where and how they live. Traditional polling methods utilized phone numbers from landlines, so they did not accurately reflect the sentiments of people using cell phones. Adding cell numbers and e-mail addresses reaches people on mobile phones and laptops, but is still not enough. Include peer-to-peer networks in your polls to capture the full context into which you are placing your message.

INTEGRATE YOUR RESEARCH AND POLLING INTO YOUR MESSAGE BOX

Let's say that your research and polling reveal that people view you as a populist and your opponent as diplomat. Your message box may look something like this:

What You Say About You	What They Say About Them
I am a populist who will fight for people.	I am a diplomat who will bring people together.
What You Say About Them	**What They Say About You**
We need a populist because some fights are necessary; if you get along with everyone, you aren't making the tough choices needed to help people.	If you fight with everyone, you can't get anything done.

The voter has a choice: a populist or a diplomat. Each candidate has strengths and weaknesses that people will take into consideration when making a choice.

So rather than just define your message as "I am a populist," you refine your message to "We need a populist because some fights are necessary; if you get along with everyone, you aren't making the tough choices needed to help people."

Once you refine your message, use the message box as a guide to keep faith with your message. For example, once you define yourself as a populist, you have committed to taking on the big fights that come up in the course of your service. This may mean taking on a sacred cow such as a corporation that employs many people in your community but does not pay living wages or provide health care to its employees.

You should use your message box periodically during the campaign to pick up on what people are saying. For example, if you are promoting a candidate as a populist and the voters are telling your phone banks that your candidate seems to back away from big fights, you will have to further refine your message.

WALK YOUR TALK

What You Say About You includes how you walk your talk. As Mahatma Gandhi famously said, you must "be the change you wish to see in the world." The clearest way to advance your message in life's day-to-day moments is to build a culture of service with your campaign.

If you are working on a political campaign or initiative campaign where the call to service is to protect and preserve the environment, start with the obvious: make your campaign carbon neutral, set up events with carpooling and public transportation, and use recycled products; then move to acts of service such as a monthly volunteer cleanup at a local park, beach, or community center. If you are campaigning on a platform of creating jobs for Americans, be sure your T-shirts and other campaign memorabilia are made in America. Every small gesture is part of a larger message. As Fred Ross Sr. used to say, "If you are able to achieve anything big in life, it's because you paid attention to the 'little' things."[11]

"People want to see how you walk on this earth," explains international human rights activist Kerry Kennedy. "Make an effort to do more than 'campaign' so that people can see who you are in your core. You can't leave that at the door for months while you are campaigning. If you do, and you get to office, there'll be some another reason you can't do it. So do something in your campaign that helps people and reflects your message." For example, her brother, former Congressman Joseph Kennedy, incorporated his message into a service: when going to senior centers to pitch health care, he would ditch the standard coffee and donuts for healthy snacks and an exercise routine of light calisthenics that he performed along with the crowd.[12]

Every communication and every action is a chance to tell your story, so be persistent and consistent in your message in all venues of the campaign. From the house meeting DVDs to the fund-raising kit to the Internet call to action to the radio ads, walk your talk to reinforce your message.

CHALLENGERS: YOUR MESSAGE EXPRESSES WHY SHOULD YOU BE HIRED

What You Say About Them may be that your opponent is out of touch. Firing people is not easy. Voters tend to stick with their decisions, so you need to make a forceful case. People watch incumbents for signs of incumbentitis. Also known as "Potomac fever" (named for the river in Washington, D.C.), incumbentitis means losing touch with your constituents or paying too much attention to the trappings of office and not the work of the job. People will be ever vigilant that you remember who you are, where you came from, why you chose to serve, and what they elected you to do for them. Once your supporters think you are in office to be something, not to do something, you will soon be out of office.

One reason to fire the incumbent may be that she is out of touch on the issues: she is in office to do something, but it hurts her constituents. For example, Chris Murphy won a Connecticut congressional race with a populist campaign against an entrenched incumbent. Though only in his early thirties, Murphy had already passed a stem cell research law in the state legislature, and as chairman of the state senate's

Public Health Committee, he had the professional stature to attack gaps in the Medicare prescription drug bill she had helped draft.

Unlike our earlier example in which a young person foolishly attacked age as a liability, Murphy concentrated on the Medicare bill and the gaps in coverage that cost Connecticut seniors money. His youth was obvious; what he stressed was his ability to deliver better care for people of all ages, not how there was anything wrong with being older. His ad "Part of the Problem" told voters that although the incumbent was a nice person, she was an enabler for an unpopular president, a divisive war, and an unfair Medicare bill.[13]

What You Say About Them may be that your opponent is a hypocrite and should not be hired. Hypocrisy is a powerful element in public service positions. The 2006 congressional races addressed this issue, notably in the context of pay raises: people who raised their own pay but not that of minimum wage workers or combat troops felt the wrath of voters. For eample, Iowa's Bruce Braley hammered his opponent on the minimum wage. The opponent, a restaurant chain owner, claimed that his employees made well in excess of $10 an hour. Yet Braley cited a waitress who said she was paid $3.09 an hour plus tips, barely bringing her pay to the minimum wage. Braley used the comparison to reinforce his message that many Iowans would benefit from a higher federal minimum wage, and to "pledge to the voters in this district that I will not accept a congressional pay increase until Congress passes a minimum wage bill."[14]

This charge cuts both ways: you should be sure that you are not vulnerable to charges of hypocrisy yourself and that you have allies to back you up if your opponent accuses you of it.

INCUMBENTS: YOUR MESSAGE DEMONSTRATES WHY YOU SHOULD BE REHIRED

What You Say About You includes why you should be re-hired. Elections for incumbents are like annual job performance reviews, only they take place on a twenty-four-hour image cycle. If you are already in office and running for re-election, your message should convey that you pay constant attention to your constituents.

Nancy Pelosi tells her House colleagues: "Your job title is your job description: representative. Be an independent voice for your district." This advice requires that you take care of all your constituents, not just the people who elected you.

"People need to know that you will provide full representation to everyone, including those who openly acknowledge that they did not vote for you," says Willie L. Brown Jr., former California Assembly Speaker and San Francisco mayor. Brown heard the call to serve during the civil rights struggle of the 1950s and was in elected office for thirty years while winning over a dozen elections himself and fielding a team of eighty legislative candidates every two years during his fifteen years as Speaker.

Having observed hundreds of candidacies, Brown advises incumbents to "define and perform your job so well that *no one but you can do it.* Whether you define the job as constituent contacts and services, perfect voting attendance, or complete knowledge of a particular subject," counsels Brown, "do your job in a unique and excellent way."[15]

Most of all, incumbents should be present in the community at every opportunity. "I should see you out and about in the community more than I see my own family," declares Brown, who kept his mayor's office in Room 200, City Hall, open to public tours all day long. "The more people who can see you are working for them, the better." [16]

REMATCH: YOUR MESSAGE MUST SHOW GROWTH, NOT A GRUDGE

If you're in a rematch, *What They Say About You* is that your repeat campaign is a grudge match. When a ballot initiative comes before the voters again and again, or two people are running against each other for the second time, it's either a grudge match or a new dynamic. If your cause or candidate was on the losing side before, the burden is on your team to create a new dynamic. Reach out to a whole new group of voters. Find as many unformed opinions as you can. Demonstrate that you are running to do something for the future, not to settle an old score. People will watch carefully to see whether your message is about your past or about their future.

Congressman John Tierney of Massachusetts ran three times against the same opponent, losing in 1994 and winning in 1996 and 1998. "Anger doesn't work," cautions Tierney, who recalls one debate early in his second race: "I came out swinging. My wife, Patrice, said 'you won this debate, but you looked mad.' Anger shows to everyone else and seriously diminishes candidate appeal. Better to identify what people liked in your campaign and highlight and improve on that." Tierney advises repeat challengers: "Do not run the last campaign. Improve your field using lessons from the last effort as to who is reliable and talented and who is not. Essentially, it is all about keeping your base from the last time and building a new voter group through concentrated outreach. We found earlier and better fund-raising possible since a core now knew us and helped us raise money."[17] The campaign successfully poured that money into get-out-the-vote efforts.

This approach was also followed by Congressman Joe Courtney of Connecticut, who ran twice for Congress, losing in 2002 and winning in 2006. In 2002, Courtney ran well but lost, 54–46 percent. Four years later, in 2006, Courtney won by approximately 83 votes out of over 242,000 cast. How did he close the margin? First, he was determined to run flat-out for two years. Second, he had family support. "I really wasn't sure what [his wife] Audrey would say again because schedules are demanding," he said in a recent profile. "But her only comment was, 'you can run, but you have to win.'"[18] Third, rather than dwell on 2002, Courtney focused on 2006 and the changing mood of the country with respect to the war and the economy. This focus on the future infused his Courtney Captains—a homegrown volunteer effort that included his supporters as well as fresh recruits from the Hilltop Brigade, a volunteer network in Connecticut.[19]

What Tierney and Courtney demonstrated was the ability to put the voters' future ahead of past setbacks and disappointments. With family support and a commitment to run again, they understood that sometimes it takes more than one interview to land the job.

THROW A PUNCH AND TAKE A PUNCH

Campaigns are tough. In the rough and tumble of politics, you have to be prepared, in the words of my grandfather, Thomas D'Alesandro Jr., to "throw a punch and take a punch." *What You Say About Them* and *What They Say About You* are the punches you have to throw and take in order to compete.

CALL TO SERVICE

MAX CLELAND

Max Cleland, Vietnam combat veteran and former Georgia senator, explains his call to service:

"I became interested in politics when I studied at American University. President Kennedy was in office, and he inspired me in many ways. In 1970, I returned to Georgia after spending a year and a half recovering from my injuries at Walter Reed Army Medical Center [Cleland lost both legs and an arm in Vietnam]. I was upset about some issues especially the war in Vietnam and the treatment of veterans returning to this country. I thought I could do a better job than the state senator in my area, so I ran against him and won. Campaigning and meeting with people got me out of the house and helped in my recovery process. An opportunity came to run for the U.S. Senate in 1996. I loved every minute of my six years in the Senate. I especially liked sitting on the Armed Services Committee, working on issues I had been passionate about for 30 years. America is great because of its people. We have a terrific entrepreneurial spirit, we believe in free government, and America is great because even a boy from a small town in Georgia can grow up and become a United States Senator."

Source: Max Cleland, "'Wire-Side' Chat with Senator Max Cleland," *Trail Mix,* April 30, 2006.

"New candidates are often shocked by the negative campaign ads they've seen on TV and in other campaigns and vow to keep theirs clean and positive," says Dotty LeMieux. She advises people not to be sidetracked by attacks. New candidates fear voters will think less of those who use negatives, even to defend themselves. They think "if I get attacked, I'll just explain the truth. The voters will understand." They won't. LeMieux says candidates should use opposition research to make pointed comparisons showing the opponent's negatives. "If you're attacked, you need to quickly respond, and then get back to your message."[20]

In 2002, Georgia Senator Max Cleland lost his seat after the opposition ran ads comparing him to terrorists. In an April 2006 "wire-side chat" for my *Trail Mix* blog, I asked Cleland about getting "swiftboated." He responded: "The biggest mistake I think we made in 2004 is that we let the accusations of the Swift Boat Veterans for Truth [that John Kerry did not earn his medals and was not a war hero] linger too long in the media."[21]

Using the message box from the Kerry campaign's perspective, you can see the dynamic of the swift boat attacks of 2004 and how a delayed response played out on the message landscape.

What You Say About You	*What They Say About Them*
Kerry: I am a war hero.	*Bush:* I will keep you safe.
What You Say About Them	*What They Say About You*
[DELAYED RESPONSE]	*Swift Boat Veterans for Truth:* John Kerry is not really a war hero.

John Kerry *is* a war hero; however, his opponents succeeded in undercutting his message by going right to the heart of his call-to-service message. If he did not defend himself quickly and decisively, could he defend America quickly and decisively? Of course he could, but that's not what his opponents were saying.

"We should have swiftly responded back as soon as the attacks appeared on the front page, and instead we underestimated the damage they caused," said Cleland, who campaigned actively for Kerry. "All future candidates should take that lesson in campaigns when they are attacked with lies and garbage."[22]

Senator Cleland backed up his words with action, helping lead the movement to establish a Democratic National Committee (DNC) veterans and military families outreach effort, campaigning for dozens of the Fighting Dems running for Congress in 2006, and speaking out quickly against attacks on U.S. Rep. John Murtha, the first Vietnam veteran elected to Congress, when Murtha was under fire for his efforts to end the Iraq War.[23] By validating the Fighting Dems' credibility on national security issues, Cleland was enhancing the *What You Say About You* element of the message; by pushing back against swiftboating attacks, Cleland was adding the *What You Say About Them* counterpunch to the debate. Hence, all four corners of the argument were engaged.

USE AGGRESSIVE SCHEDULING TO ADVANCE YOUR MESSAGE

Your message box drives your schedule. Prioritize every action with the highest scrutiny: How does this event help advance the message of the campaign? If you are taking the lead in a public service campaign as a manager or candidate, with time being of the essence, nearly every event in your day must be subject to the strictest scrutiny: Why am I here? What votes are here? How does this event help me advance my message? Who will be impressed by my decision to attend or offended by my decision to send one of my allies as a surrogate?

Be consistent. Every event should be consistent with your message. If you say you are a populist but you are only delivering speeches in venues that cost money to attend you are undermining your own message. On the other hand, don't go overboard and deliver your support-the-troops message in a tank. Keep it real.

Create events that help the campaign meet its message goals. A successful schedule is one where every event maximizes your messaging goals. To take our veterans example, if you are campaigning in support of veterans and military families, you should deliver your message with members of your veterans and military families advisory group, at the house meeting or town hall, with members of a veterans service organization in attendance.

Refresh, reinforce, and repeat your message. Participate in an online chat or radio interview after the meeting, send the message out to your e-mail lists of supporters and media contacts, and repeat it.

Concurrent events. There will almost certainly come a day when two important events take place at the same time. Campaign staff will be evenly divided about which event can be skipped. No one will want to compromise. So which event goes on the schedule? The answer lies in consulting the message box to decide which event best advances your message.

Only the scheduler puts events on the calendar. Otherwise, there will be chaos. Schedulers are not calendar keepers; they are message managers. Schedulers must process dozens of requests and keep track of a million details. A well-organized scheduler will see to it that all requests are confirmed or denied in writing with a simple card and that information on every event is filed for possible future use. Detailed information is needed on each event accepted, including the exact time the event starts, who will attend, who will speak, and how the message will be advanced through press coverage of the event.

"Are your scheduling eyes bigger than your logistical stomach?" Andrew Cuomo, Clinton-Gore secretary of Housing and Urban Development, once posed this question in a staff meeting, and I've been using it as a guideline for public service campaigns ever since. Cuomo wanted to make sure that we were not trying to do too much, leaving little margin for preparation time. A good scheduler shows compassion for the campaign team: there has to be room for food, sleep, exercise, and worship. Without a minimum of rest and reflection, no one is at their best. Better to identify fewer events and do them well than to overbook and underperform.

Using the message box to shape your message and your campaign events will create invaluable venues to connect with people.

GET REAL: DRAW YOUR MESSAGE BOX

What You Say About You—put your best case forward.

What They Say About Them—put their best case forward.

What You Say About You	What They Say About Them
What You Say About Them	What They Say About You

What You Say About Them—why are you better and/or why are they worse?

What They Say About You—their best case against you and/or why are they better than you?

Integrate your call to service, track record, allies, research, polling, and common sense into your message box.

As you draw your message box, engage your allies. Consider:

- Who should say your message?
- Who should talk about the opposition?
- Who should back up your message once you are under attack?

Once you draw your message box, be sure your message is consistent. Consider:

- How do I build a culture of service in my campaign to reinforce and repeat my message?
- How does my schedule advance my message?

FIVE

Connect with People

"You talkin' to me?"
—Taxi Driver

Most Americans spend only a few minutes out of their week thinking about politics and public policy. To make your message fit into a small sliver of attention, you must repeat it again and again. You always have competition—not from your opponent but from the messages people are already receiving. You have to cut through the clutter—on television it's your ad versus their favorite show; in the mailbox it's your mailer versus the Pottery Barn catalog. So you have to reach people speaking their language, not yours. You need your message to be everywhere possible so that there is a chance that it can get through.

SHOW UP: REACH PEOPLE WHERE THEY LIVE

"In Montana, our messaging had not been personal. We were using political jargon, and it wasn't appealing to regular peo-

ple who don't speak like politicians," recalls Brad Martin, who
served as the longtime executive director of the Montana
Democratic Party. "So we started to think of our voters as the
people who went to our convenience store, where the sign in
the window advertises 'beer ice ammo' for sale."[1] He continued, "Rather than direct our remarks to political people, we
thought of them as beer ice ammo people. We said *general
fund* and beer ice ammo people said 'Huh?' We switched to
balancing the legislature's checkbook and beer ice ammo people responded, 'Oh I get it,' because no one has a general fund
at home but nearly everyone has a checkbook."[2]

Showing up takes planning. Martin reflects on how the
Montana team came together and reversed years of losses:
"Luck is the domain of the well prepared. We won elections
only after learning to work together as a team." In a lesson for
future leaders everywhere, Martin observes: "We had to get
together, pull all the bolts out of the car and determine what
was and was not working. We did this every two years, bringing more and more people to the table. Early on, former Congressman Pat Williams helped promote our Native American
outreach, providing resources directly to the reservations for
peer-to-peer contact and persuasion efforts. We also reached
out to the pro-choice community, the hunting and fishing
community, and folks from the labor movement."[3]

This comprehensive outreach strategy in Montana started
in a convenience store and has helped elect Democratic Governor Brian Schweitzer in 2004, Senator Jon Tester in 2006,
and a legion of state legislators since its inception.

To connect with people, you have to bring in every potential ally from your community inventory, empower them to
build support among their networks, and advance your message in every corner of your community. It may take months

if not years of disciplined organizing, but eventually the results will pay off when people receive your message and join your cause.

MIND YOUR APPEARANCE AND ETIQUETTE

Be appropriate for the audience. If you are going to a low-income neighborhood, avoid wearing your fancy suit. Don't wear wingtips to the fish fry or the ballyard. Through proper dress, you send the immediate message that you care enough about your cause to be well groomed yet down-to-earth. Avoid clothes with distracting patterns and dangly jewelry. Avoid flip-flops (the footwear and the policy switches). Dress with the professionalism, care, and respect that you would for a job interview.

Give yourself an honest examination of your personal habits. Do you forget some basic manners, like saying please and thank-you? Do you fail to look people in the eye when you talk to them or when they talk to you? Do you bite your nails in public? These types of habits may show a lack of confidence, which you can amend through training. Practice a speech on videotape. Watch yourself. Then tape it again. You will see your strengths and weaknesses. Watch your posture, keep your hands close to the table or podium, and don't forget to breathe while answering a question.

"Once you are on, you are on," says Andrea Dew Steele, founder of Emerge America, a grassroots women's training network. Steele tells aspiring women leaders, "You are the leader no matter where you are."[4] People will constantly measure the way you relate to the public, potential donors, reporters, and volunteers.

SPEAK OUT

Once you decide you want to assert yourself as a community leader, consider your public service to be your interview. Whether by taking a risk, managing a crisis, or speaking on a larger platform, people have to see you in the job in order to determine if you are up to it. Give interviews, do town hall meetings, attend debates—whatever you can do to "interview" for the job.

When you speak for your cause, always start by making your pitch. Be clear, speaking in language that can be easily understood by people from all different backgrounds. Be concise, using no more than seventy-five words to get your message across. Be consistent, repeating the values you want to get across. Be convincing, by linking an issue to a value with a personal story with morals that evoke your political principles. And be humble, always asking people to vote for you or your cause and thanking them for their consideration.

Give people a reason to come on board. Lezlee Westine says that when recruiting for TechNet, she begins every meeting by making the pitch. "People expect the vision, goals, team, tactics, strategy, and early adopters," says Westine, who adds that with respect to the venture capital industry, "a good qualified team that has been successful" is key to the presentation being well received.[5] Advocating for political candidates and causes is similar: mention endorsements by individuals, organizations, and interest groups.

The greatest sign of respect for yourself, your vision, and your audience is your level of advance work. When my four siblings and I were growing up, our mom's theory of homework was, "Proper preparation prevents poor performance." The same holds true for public service. You need to prepare.

If you are appearing on television, watch a few episodes and interviews so that you understand the flavor of the show. If you are going on radio, listen to the show in advance. Comedian and commentator Will Durst used to cohost the *Will and Willie Show* on Air America in San Francisco. He and cohost Willie L. Brown Jr. had features such as "Burst of Durst" or "What Would Willie Do?" "People who made a reference to our features got extra points in our book," says Durst. "We talked about them before and after they were on the show, so it helped their cause to show us and the audience that they were listening before they came on."[6]

Remember, the microphone is always on. Whether you are at a debate, on the radio, or at a speech, you must stay on message. Avoid jokes, off-the-cuff comments, and insults. A cautionary tale is former Senator George Allen's 2006 "macaca moment." Allen used the term *macaca* to describe a campaign tracker (a young man of Indian descent tracking Allen's campaign movements with a video camera). The young man made a vlog (a video blog) of Allen making the slur, Allen's opponents used viral marketing to blog and vlog that moment virally across the blogosphere and into the mainstream media spotlight. Allen never fully apologized and never full recovered—losing to Democrat Jim Webb. [7]

If you are volunteering for a nonprofit organization or for a political campaign, appear on behalf of your cause at community forums or as a surrogate in house meetings and debates. If you are a candidate running for office, look for an opportunity to address the media as a representative of your political party. For instance, in 2006 several congressional candidates were given the opportunity to present the national Democratic response to the president's radio address. In so doing, they elevated themselves and their causes: Iraq veterans Tammy Duckworth and Patrick Murphy on Iraq, child advocate Patty Wetterling on the House page scandal, consumer attorney Bruce Braley on Social Security privatization, and energy expert Jerry McNerney on ethics, energy, and Iraq. Find the venues where people see or hear debates, show up, and speak out for your cause or candidate.

LISTEN: KEEP AN OPEN FEEDBACK LOOP

An effective public servant listens to what people are saying for both the good news, such as community support for candidates and causes, and bad news, such as discontent and in some cases outright rebellion. An open feedback loop means that you put information out to people, people respond with feedback, you process their feedback, you lock in positives and adjust negatives, and then you send information back out. With the kitchen cabinet, you will get the bad news one way or another. The challenge is to mechanize how feedback comes to you and how your reinforcements or rebuttals go back out. The responsibility for a campaign worker is to make sure that the feedback you receive on the phones or in the neighborhoods is reported to the campaign leadership, and that you get information in response that you can bring back to voters.

Two political election examples demonstrate that listening to people will reveal the political moment, especially when voters are angry, and that elected officials who do not respond head-on will become former elected officials.

Public anger that crescendoed into a California gubernatorial recall of Gray Davis in 2003 was palpable even before the election of 2002. In October 2002, as we were phone-banking for soon-to-be Congressman Dennis Cardoza in Stockton,

California, we were met with outbursts by people angry at how negative the statewide races were and at how ads were merely personal attacks, not substantive plans to get California out of debt. Though we explained that we were calling on behalf of a congressional candidate, not a statewide race, voters were insistent on venting their anger before they agreed to hear our pitch for Cardoza. By February, activists were holding bake sales on the steps of the state capitol selling slices of "upside-down-priorities cake" to protest the budget fee increases and their disproportionate impact on families struggling to get by.

Thus it came as little surprise in October 2003, when our phone-banking into South Los Angeles on the anti-recall campaign revealed angry voters telling us *to the penny* just how much more they were paying to the Department of Motor Vehicles for a car registration fee that Davis had tripled. The wave of voter anger—from an election campaign people felt was not about them, to a budget they thought was unfair to them, to a recalled governor—was a yearlong sweep of frustration that set the stage for electing a Republican governor, Arnold Schwarzenegger, and changed the course of California history.

Similarly, in 2005 many people expressed their frustration over Republican handling of the Iraq war and the culture of corruption that was costing people personally, such as with higher prices at the pump and the pharmacy. This time the Democrats listened. As Rahm Emanuel, at the time Democratic Congressional Campaign Committee chairman, repeatedly said of the strategy: "We have the three *R*s: (1) Recruit candidates to run against ethically challenged Republicans, in open seats of retiring Republicans, and in districts where Bush won by close margins in 2004; (2) Retain incumbent Democrats with strong defense and a national message; and (3) Respond rapidly to swiftboat style attacks."[8]

By summertime, the Democrats were proposing a New Direction for America on economic and war issues,[9] while the Republicans had a stay-the-course position in Iraq and an American Values Agenda touching on gambling, abortion, guns, religion, a proposed constitutional amendment to ban gay marriage, and a prohibition on human cloning.[10] In November 2006 angry voters chose economic and war issues and again changed the course of history.

Both election examples demonstrate the need to listen to people and to provide change before they provide it for you. The lesson here: when you call your members or poll your voters or convene community meetings with your neighbors, you won't always get what you expect to hear. Be prepared to listen. Use the message-box technique to help figure out where your message needs clarity and whether or not people are with you. Perhaps what people are saying about you is not what you anticipated before you called them. Perhaps your negatives are stronger than you thought.

Good listening works for candidates and causes. If, for instance, you are working with a nonprofit that decides to increase membership fees, your pledge drive might reveal angry people who do not want to pay the increase. In that case, you may have to step back, reflect on why the increase is needed, and do as much belt-tightening as you can. Then go back to your members with a fuller explanation of how raising their fees was a last resort, taken after everyone involved with the nonprofit tightened their belts, and how raising their fees will ultimately result in a stronger nonprofit performing more effective public service.

Whatever your specifics, the general rule is to reinforce or readjust as necessary and to make sure people know that you listened, you heard, and you responded respectfully.

DEVELOP A MESSAGE COMMUNICATIONS PLAN WITH A BALANCED MEDIA MIX

Every campaign for a cause or a candidate needs a message communications plan that provides the nuts-and-bolts strategy to connect with people and persuade them to support you.

A good message communications plan is a calendar that matches your paid media (mailers, radio spots, and television commercials) to your free media (press conferences and news coverage). In matching the free and paid media, you are attempting to create a wave of information that will wash over the community. This means that people should hear your radio ad calling for people to join your community organization on the same day that they receive a solicitation in the mail from a high-profile community leader praising your organization and urging new members to sign up. Or if you are working on a political campaign, people should see your candidate's press conference about cleaning up a hazardous waste site on the same evening as they see your paid TV commercial about your candidate's environmental record.

A message communications plan requires a clear statement of your objectives: get the message out to connect with people identified in the community inventory as being likely to support you as many times as possible to get critical masses of them to support you.

You also need a schedule of when the paid media will air on radio and television and when the mail will land in people's homes, as well as an overall schedule of free press activities. Free press activities should be grouped into message weeks, or issue weeks, during which the campaign tries to communicate a particular piece of information to people. Most important, your communications plan should fit together as a package.

Your campaign kickoff event introduces your message to people. Different parts of this message are presented to people during the following weeks through free press events and message weeks. Paid media advertising reminds people of the argument you are making. Then, in the final days of the campaign, your free and paid media should come together and make it clear to people that you have proved your argument. At the start say what you are going to do (hold one hundred house meetings, conduct a listening tour, visit every community, collect ten thousand signed petitions for your initiative). Then do it.

People need to hear your message many times before they can absorb it. Your communications effort will be more successful with five mail pieces than with a radio spot that airs only five times, yet the costs of each might be about the same. The key is to vary your communications tools to design a "layered" communications plan that takes advantage of the strengths of each different medium: newspapers, broadcast television, local cable, viral marketing, community weeklies, blogs, vlogs, radio billboards, mail, phone banks, and texting.

The challenge for aspiring public servants is twofold: (1) build a culture of service in your organizations and candidate campaigns, and (2) reach out to as many venues as you can to convey your message. Each of these elements is important; the goal is a balanced media mix that brings news to people they way they prefer to receive it and that talks to people the way they talk to one another.

Broadcast television. Broadcast television is where most people are accustomed to receiving their information. Television has the ability to reach millions of voters with a unified message, and reaching these numbers is critical in most large campaigns. If you have the money to dominate television, do it. But, never forget that buying a few commercials is a waste of money. You must go in for the whole program if you are going to be effective.

Cable television. Cable television provides many of the same benefits of broadcast television. It is cheaper, and you can target your spending on those cable networks that serve only viewers in your community. In fact, specific neighborhoods can be targeted according to which cable provider they use. Few media institutions reach across the entire political bandwidth, so you will have to broadcast your message in different venues to be sure you are reaching everyone. Ethnic media are also crucial: for example, about half of Latino voters are under the age of forty, and on average Latinos are ten years younger than their non-Hispanic counterparts.[11]. Thus, Spanish-language media is another key venue in which to get your message across.

Radio. Radio is an extremely cost-effective medium by which to connect with people. Syndicated radio host Bill Press observes, "Fewer and fewer people read newspapers or watch TV news. Especially for politically active people, talk radio has a *huge* influence on what people think and how people vote. It also presents a *huge* opportunity for influencing public opinion, building public awareness and support, getting the message out, getting people to participate. Witness the massive immigration rallies driven by talk radio."[12]

Your message communications plan needs a strategy for radio that includes ads, audio releases, and live air time.

Radio ads. Check your local listings as well as national talk show resources like Talkers.com (the Web site of *Talkers* magazine) to determine the content of your radio stations and to decide which ones to target. Talkers.com posts radio content and audience information in online features such as "The Week in Review," "The 100 Most Important Radio Talk Show Hosts in America (the Heavy Hundred)," and "The Top Talk Radio Audiences." You will find that conservatives have saturated talk radio. A 2007 Center for American Progress report shows that there are ten hours of conservative talk offered for every one hour of progressive talk. Of the 257 talk stations owned by the five largest companies, 92 percent, or 236, broadcast not a single minute of progressive talk.[13]

You can use this information to send a more targeted message to stations that carry syndicated conservative or progressive talk shows. Or if you are buying radio time on a local station that carries the home baseball team or on a local outlet of ESPN radio, you may choose a sports-related theme or advocate for your cause or candidate. Your message communications plan should include ads on radio stations with broad audiences in ethnic communities; for example, the plan might include buying ads on Spanish-language radio. Knowing the message environment into which you are sending ads or audio releases, or are seeking live airtime, will help you map out your message communications plan and budget your resources for maximum impact.

Radio ads are much cheaper than television ads, so you can buy large numbers of ads and dominate the airwaves for days at a time. These types of saturation buys are effective at motivating people to support your candidate or cause. One creative use of radio ads is the purchase of ads for a radio station's traffic and weather reports, since listeners tend to tune in for them at designated times every hour.

Audio releases. You can also get your message out by purchasing an MP3 player or computer software and recording public service announcements, commentary on issues, or reactions to a major news event. You can then e-mail the MP3 files to local radio stations as audio press releases. Although still canned, the releases do give you an opportunity to read your announcement or commentary in your own voice, and they help you connect with radio listeners.

Live airtime. Bill Press advises aspiring leaders to "listen to what's on the air" so they know the message environment, to call to inform the discussion with your message, and to book your most persuasive people as guests on talk radio. "Remember: producers have two to three hours to fill every day; they're always looking for strong, lively, provocative, well-informed experts on hot topics of day."[14]

Blogs. Your main way to communicate with people online is through a blog you establish and through postings you make on community blogs that can distribute your message and ideas to Internet activists, that can thank and update your supporters, and that can attract new people to your effort.

Every organization, candidate, or campaign should have a blog that records their activities and that calls others to service. An index or site map on your Web site should include your biography, mission statement, vision, ideas and values, service résumé, community maps and information, speeches and interviews, event news that is refreshed in real time, and streaming downloads. Invite volunteers to sign up online to join your effort or ask them to take your message or candidate to their neighbors, either by going door-to-door or by hosting a house meeting. Set up events in every corner of your community, and alert people by e-mail and through a centralized calendar as to when they can join you for house meetings, visibility activities, door-knocking, and other events. Be sure to showcase photos from across the community to demonstrate the broad support and positive energy of your campaign.

Blogging also means expanding your Web presence to online communities. "Thousands of bloggers enable campaigns to circumvent mainstream media and create stories and attention that might otherwise go unnoticed," says Lezlee Westine.[15]

Know your Web audience. As discussed in chapter 2, Know Your Community, blogs have individual community structures and topics. Many bloggers are distrustful of the mainstream media and strive to create their own message environment. *Daily Kos* founder Markos Moulitsas explains: "Unlike the past when a few select media organizations and political leaders acted as gatekeepers for information and action, now there are thousands of such gatekeepers. Sites like *Daily Kos* work independently of those old gatekeepers, deciding for themselves what sort of issues they want to work for."[16]

Recent studies have examined the demographics of the blogosphere, finding that many of those surveyed leaned toward progressives and strong liberal positions. The Pew Internet and American Life Survey published in January 2007 calculated that 46 percent of Internet users—or 31 percent of the entire adult population—used the Internet for some kind of political purpose during the last election. Twenty percent (of that 31 percent) got news and information about the campaign from blogs. About 6 percent of the nation's adult population, or thirteen to fourteen million people, used the political blogosphere for campaign information in 2006. These people had a statistically meaningful preference for Democratic candidates: 52 percent of them voted for the Democratic candidates, while 35 percent voted for Republicans.[17] The 2006 blogads.com political blogs reader survey showed that among respondents the biggest group of blog readers was wealthy white males. Nearly 49 percent of the respondents identified themselves as Democrats.[18]

Blogging also means outreach to Internet sites that are getting people engaged in politics. If you work with a nonprofit, you may find it difficult to garner mainstream media coverage for your cause, and you may never be able to afford television advertising, so take a cue from political campaigns and start with bloggers rather than mainstream media reporters. A direct message to a sympathetic audience can create buzz and perhaps attract the mainstream media to your cause.

If you are Internet savvy, you may wish to join the "mashup" fun—uploading raw files and mashing that content up to create your own ads and video spots. For instance, Yahoo! bought Junk Cut so their software allows mashups (with firewalls so campaigns can OK "their" ads). All told, there are 130 million Yahoo.com users, which means a fertile ground for civic and political discourse.[19] Yahoo! and *Slate* teamed up with the *Huffington Post* to create a presidential mashup service. In what Arianna Huffington calls "campaign 2008 meets the brave new world of interactivity," users send questions, candidates will respond, and users will be able to program their own vlogs compiled of selected responses.[20]

Other online domains that invite your participation include YouTube, Meetup, Facebook, MySpace, Friendster, and LinkedIn. These are places where you can post ads and information for you and your cause.

Finally, monitor popular blogs: review blogs that oppose your ideas for early warning signals of voter discontent or political attacks, and run banner ads on targeted blogs to drive people to your Web site.

Vlogs. Vlogs of your presentations should be available on your Web site as a video résumé. If you are working with a cause, include your members giving testimonials (for example, "why I joined the union," "why I am fighting for universal health care," "my personal commitment to fight global warming," "why my family will benefit from stem cell research"). If you are working with a campaign, your vlogs should spotlight volunteers and supporters of an issue or candidate (for example, "why my family supports this school bond," "why as a veteran I am endorsing this candidate for office").

Keep it real—the more personal the better. Include personal appeals on your donations page from the nonprofit board member, pledge drive chairperson, or candidate. Cross-post in as many venues (YouTube, and so forth) as possible and be sure that your blog has a full vlog inventory of your public service. As you embrace technology, also accept that technology is capturing you: everything you say or do can be recorded by the simplest cell phone camera and vlogged. Live accordingly. Accept that your movements will be recorded for posterity and be polite to your trackers (videographers sent by the opposition to record your movements).

Viral marketing. Named for the way viruses are spread from one person directly to another, viral marketing an inexpensive way to share news about your cause or campaign. Even cheaper than broadcast or cable television, viral marketing allows you to produce an ad, post it on your Web site and on file-sharing Web sites like YouTube, e-mail it to your supporters and urge them to share it with their friends, and send it as a video press release to the media. Ideally, you will create buzz on broadcast television about an ad that you could never afford to advertise in that medium. Similarly, you could do the same viral marketing for a very modest cable TV buy. The key here is to activate your social networks to literally spread your ad to their e-mail lists, so that you generate as many hits as possible. This buzz in turn may generate a news story as well as another success you can report back to your networks. Take the macaca moment: a story about George Allen's insult may have made an impact—but the video was virally marketed from vlog to vlog and blog to blog until the buzz was so intense that it permeated all coverage of the campaign. There was simply no escaping it.

Newspapers. Newspapers carry weight with their readers. The Newspaper Association of America Web site (www.naa .org) indicates that three of four voters are regular newspaper readers and that one of two undecided voters look to newspapers in making up their minds about how to vote on election days.[21] Thus, newspapers are perfect for making serious arguments on an issue—promoting your vision (or taking apart the opposition) point by point. In addition, small community newspapers can sometimes be useful in reaching people interested in local news.

Opinion makers, reporters, politicians, community leaders, and large campaign contributors tend to be regular newspaper readers. A good newspaper ad can create a buzz in these small circles. That buzz, in turn, can help create more positive media coverage and can motivate supporters to do more.

Start with your local paper. Many newspapers have sections
that differentiate by geographical zones. A balanced media
mix must include online ads, in-paper ads, newspaper pack-
aging inserts, or ads on the plastic delivery bags themselves
that allow you to target your message to the zip codes of certain paper routes.

Community weeklies. Community weeklies and alternative
media venues are often the most successful for emerging
leaders. Network TV, major blogs and radio, and even local papers will be the venue of political campaigns for president and
of state campaigns with national implications, so the majority
of emerging leaders and potential campaign workers will
likely not get television coverage. Even if you "earn" your
media with a powerful visual, not everyone watches the
nightly news or picks up the local daily paper, so many people
may miss your major media moment. People's lives are busy,
and family and work come first. Furthermore, people may
choose to get most of their information from a community
source. Therefore, you must make a sincere effort to reach out
to people through the venues that they seek out for information. Leave no stone unturned in trying to get your campaign
events featured in community publications: church bulletins,
senior center bulletins, and newsletters published by neighborhood groups. Many will welcome your additions. The
weeklies have their own special publication schedules. Many
print midweek, so you must determine deadlines. They are
free, local to neighborhoods, and are read cover to cover. Don't
miss this opportunity.

Billboards. Billboards can be effective for challengers or organizations with little or no name recognition—depending
on size and location. It may be fun for candidates to buy the

billboard across from your opponent's campaign office, but only do it if you have money to spare. Otherwise, mail, radio, and blogging are much more cost-effective.

Direct mail. Direct mail is inexpensive and effective, making it the medium most organizations and campaigns use to get their messages out. You can target direct mail at a particular audience more effectively than with any other medium. Voters are accustomed to receiving information in the mail, so they naturally pay attention to your message. Mail also allows you to send a specific message to a group of voters who care most about that issue. Be aware that your direct mail should be sent to people whom your community inventory microtargeting and local wisdom have identified as receptive to your message.

Phone banks. Phone banks can allow you to reach people in their homes, find out their opinions on your issue or campaign, and then follow up, encouraging supportive voters to go out and vote and pushing undecided voters to take another look at your issue or candidate. Phones are a great vehicle for getting people to attend a house meeting or community activity, or for getting them out to vote, because you can contact them on Election Day. In low turnout elections, this type of concerted effort can make a big difference.

Texting. Texting people with messages to their cell phones is especially appropriate for young people, who use texting and instant messaging rather than laptops and desktops to communicate with their friends. Most new-media vendors now have inexpensive ways for you to send action alerts to people informing them about upcoming events and urging them to RSVP to events or to show their support for a cause or candidate. With a simple *Reply*, people can text a message that will result in a computer-generated petition to a politician on an issue. After an action has been completed, a follow-up text can express thanks and share results.

Balance your media. As you choose the elements of your media mix, consider how people in your community receive their information. That will drive your strategy. If you are not Web savvy but your community is, you will need a good tutorial. Whichever mix you choose, remember that in each instance you should consider your presentation with the essential public speaking advice: know your audience, connect with people, and talk to them the way they talk to one another.

WORK WITH THE MEDIA

Interacting with the media is essential to communicating with people. Three rules of thumb: respect media deadlines; present your message, not a script; and do not lie.

First, respect media deadlines. A journalist's job is to get the news out, and your job is to get your message across. You must both do your jobs within certain time constraints. For television, everyone from the fact-checker to the anchorperson operates within the daily news cycle. This cycle starts in the morning and runs all day, until the final reporter files their story and the last television newscast ends. To get good coverage by the media, you must work within their deadlines; they will generally not work within yours. For example, if a print reporter has to file a story by 5 p.m. and you do not call back with a comment until 5:30 p.m., you are most likely not going to be in print the next day.

Understand the news cycle and dominate the news of the day. Any news worth making or charge worth responding to

PRESS CONFERENCE CHECKLIST

✓ Location must fit your message. If you are talking about home-lessness, go stand in front of a homeless shelter. Be careful not to make the media travel long distances.

✓ Check the location in advance before calling the press confer-ence. Visit the site at the same time of day you will hold the press conference to be sure there is nothing to distract the press from your story.

✓ Visual content must be TV friendly. To compete with wars, fires, and floods, you need outstanding visuals. Time the event well. Avoid press conferences on Sunday (unless necessary) or after 3 p.m.

✓ Work out the speaking order before the press conference is an-nounced. Setting the order will eliminate awkward confusion in front of the microphone.

✓ Call reporters a day in advance and give them a hint about what you are doing the next day. They will appreciate the notice.

✓ Make a second round of pitch calls on the morning of the event. Check with the stations to find out which ones are sending cameras.

✓ Practice answering tough questions that may come up.

✓ Make sure there is a podium present, and anything else you re-quire to make your statement.

✓ Have something for reporters to hang microphones on if you don't have a podium.

✓ Follow up with reporters after your event is over.

is worth responding to in the same news cycle as when it was made. Online journalists and new-media bloggers may have even tighter deadlines, so be aware that respecting journalists' time is essential to a good working relationship.

Second, present your message, not a script. The more automatic your answers, the more people will tune you out or try to trip you up. Either way, you will have lost an opportunity to express your passion for your call to service. Reporters will be looking for your personality, your response to pressure, and evidence of your work for people. Political reporters are particularly attuned to the "do you want to do something or do you want to be something?" question because they continuously cover people who grow attached to the ego and fame associated with power and can sniff out hypocrisy pretty quickly.

Phil Matier and Andy Ross write the eponymous "Matier and Ross" column in the *San Francisco Chronicle*, covering local and state politics. They advise that you should not run for office until you can identify "the comma behind your name"—that is, what you have done for people.[22] Just announcing that you have money and values and vision without presenting a track record will automatically place you at a disadvantage. You must communicate a reason for running that is larger than yourself and be prepared to tell how you helped people.

Third, know that at some point in every campaign, the "oh no call" is going to come from the media. It may be something you anticipate, like a past mistake you have already shared with your campaign leadership team, something you may have gotten an early warning about from your phone-banking, or something you never saw coming.

In any event, the phone is ringing. If you have one, your

press aide should be taking the call and scheduling a response. If you need time, say so. Take some time to consult with your kitchen cabinet. But you cannot put off the inevitable. You have to respect the deadline, return the call, and DO NOT LIE.[23]

The reporter is making a judgment about you as a human being: Are you a good person who has made a mistake as humans do and will fess up, come clean, apologize, and move on, or are you someone who is going to lie? "This is the worst time for a reporter to dislike you," cautions Brad Martin.[24]

Voters don't expect you to be perfect, but they do expect you to be honest. Matier and Ross advise: "Face it and tell it: meet the questions head-on, don't overspin, and don't be afraid to be right." When muckrakers call, remember: "This isn't the end of the world." Step outside of yourself. Make as full a disclosure as you can. Your cause will matter more than a mistake you made.

Consider, Matier advises, the list of "negatives" about Abraham Lincoln—inexperienced, financial problems, troubled marriage, bouts of depression—yet Lincoln's political narrative as Honest Abe, who was going to put an end to the Civil War and slavery was ultimately more compelling to the American people.[25]

PREPARE FOR DEBATES

As you assert leadership in a public service effort, you may be called upon to represent your cause or candidate in a debate. Debates are the rare venues in a campaign in which the outcome is not entirely predictable. Political debates have gone from freewheeling policy discussions in the last century to carefully scripted twenty-first-century television events. Thus, it was considered significant when Bill Clinton left his podium at a 1992 debate and walked out in front of the audience to speak with the guests more closely. The very compactness of debates means there is more room for that type of symbolic gesture.[26]

If you are a leader on an issue, your personal style will be assessed through the prism of the underlying themes of your cause. For example, if you are active in your local school board and you step up to debate whether a particular book should be taught to children of certain ages, consider your tone and prepare your facts: what the book's place is in the curriculum, whether the book is being taught in other school districts, whether there is room for compromise, and what the nature of the decision-making process is. If you come across as angry or unprepared, you will not make your best case for the measured, educated position you want your community to take.

When negotiating debate format, think of your message and the best way to convey it. Let's say you are negotiating on behalf of a candidate for office. If she is comfortable with crowds, push for a town hall meeting format. If she is shorter than the others in the forum, press for a seated round table discussion. If she is the most knowledgeable on the issues, you may refuse to allow notes in the debate. The smallest detail should be negotiated in favor of getting your message across.

Many people practice hours of debate preparation, simulating as much as possible the setting of the actual debate, using friends or volunteers to play the moderator and the opposition. This aggressive preparation is always helpful, so if you are the one in the spotlight, overcome any resistance to practice, and discipline yourself to prepare. Now that debates are being broadcast and Webcast, with questions posed by viewers and online contributors, surf the Web in advance and prepare yourself for the curveball question.

Once the debate has started, respond to each question, enlarge the issue in your response, and then take the answer back to your message. If you are asked a divisive question, George Lakoff advises, you should say so. "Be ready for questions presupposing your opponent's frames," he warns. "Rather than answer a question that essentially asks 'when did you stop beating your wife?' call it out: 'that question is designed to be divisive.' Then, go on to make your point."[27]

As with all media appearances, know the moderator and the audience. Come prepared to make some news—either about yourself or the opposition. Then hammer away at your message throughout the debate. Everyone on stage is there to make news at someone else's expense, so be ready for an attack and keep on message. Stay on message even during breaks: remember, "The microphone is always on." Follow up with a press statement underlining your message.

ENGAGE YOUR SUPPORTERS TO INTERACT WITH THE MEDIA

One step that you can take at any given moment to serve your cause is to take simple actions to put forth your views on local media outlets and respond to misinformation that advances a biased story line.

Your Web site should list media outlets, e-mail addresses, fax and phone information so that your supporters can communicate your message and monitor media coverage of your efforts. Display action alerts (urging supporters to speak out) and success stories (the results of any letters published or calls aired on your blog).

Write a letter to the editor. Letters to the editor are opinion pieces, so make sure your first sentence states your point of view. Make your letter short (two hundred words or fewer) and to the point. Newspapers will sometimes edit your letter down to as few as three sentences, so make sure each sentence is relevant to the letter's overall point. Newspapers often specify what information they need in order to publish a letter, so be sure your letter includes that information.

You should also include your contact information (full name, address, telephone number, and e-mail address). Newspapers will often contact writers before they publish their letters to ensure the letters are genuine. Newspapers typically publish letters with the author's name and home town (for example: "Jane Doe, Chicago"), so make sure whatever you say in your letter is something you would feel comfortable saying aloud in a room full of your friends and neighbors.

Call in to a radio show. "Callers drive talk radio," says Bill Press. He advises campaigns to "use talk radio to get the facts straight, reinforce your message, and let the community know what's going on and how to get involved."[28]

If you are the caller, remember Will Durst's advice and listen to a show before you call in to get a feel for what the hosts cover and the tone of their show. Call in to a show as early in the time slot as you can. If the line is busy, wait a few seconds and try again. Most radio shows have far more callers than can be accommodated on the air.

Write down your question or comment ahead of time so that if you do go on the air, you are prepared. Before you go on the air, you will briefly talk with a "screener." The screener works in the radio station and, as the name implies, helps the radio host select calls that will be appropriate and entertaining. The screener will ask your name, location, phone number, and the topic of your call.

Make sure the topic of your call is clear and concise, keep it short and be polite. Also be in the moment—if you are interrupted before you can complete your point or question, kindly but firmly say, "Please let me finish my point." Stay calm, concise, and clear—regardless of how the host responds to your point or question.

Monitor media bias. David Brock, who leads the watchdog organization Media Matters of America, enumerates elements of bias to look out for: distortions, errors, and misstatements; unbalanced coverage; misleading arguments; uncritical reporting; lack of coverage; repeating partisan talking points; and, extreme commentary. Although Media Matters' mission is to combat conservative misinformation, the following tools and tactics recommended by Brock may be used by anyone regardless of where you define yourself on the philosophical spectrum.[29]

Send a specific critique. Be polite. Keep it short. Be specific. The person who reads your e-mail should come away with a clear understanding of your request. Do you think an issue has received too little attention? Has an important viewpoint been excluded from a story? Make sure the subject line of your message conveys what you are writing about. For example, write "Your October 6 article on taxes uses incorrect information" instead of "tax issues." Personalize your e-mail—but don't get personal. Each e-mail should be directed to one individual or media outlet and should refer to the coverage (or lack thereof) of that particular individual or outlet.

Contact advertisers. If a news outlet has a habit of presenting misinformation, contact companies that financially support or advertise on it and request they withdraw their support. Identify the companies whose advertisements appear most often, or visit the news outlet's Web site to determine who provides financial support.

Get active locally. If there is a particular news reporter, radio host, or television personality in your community who presents misinformation or fails to balance political views, start your own campaign to draw attention to any misrepresentation of the truth. Many individual activists use Web sites to draw attention to those who spread false and misleading information in their local media markets. Search for local or state blogs that critique the media that could be an excellent source for information or a great potential ally.[30]

RENEW YOUR CONNECTION WITH FOLLOW-UP AND THANK-YOUS

With every communication, be sure to ask for support (membership, dollars, votes), direct people back to your Web site, and thank them for their consideration. Then follow up with results of their work. "People want feedback on the success of what they've done," says Kerry Kennedy. "If you send a thank-you letter, they're committed. There should never be a time when people aren't thanked and recognized for past achievement and asked to participate in the next. If they never hear from you, you've lost them," she warns.[31]

Announcing the results—members joined, precincts walked, house meetings held, signatures collected, money raised, hits on a vlog, or texts for a cause—lets people know that their actions served a purpose and resulted in making a difference. Even if you did not reach your stated goals, remind people that you challenged them to service and that their actions were appreciated and meaningful. Letting people know results is not only good manners but good organizing: it will keep people engaged and invested in your efforts. People who did not participate in one action may see the results of another and be inspired to act next time.

Follow-ups and thank-yous renew your connection with people and help them see the power of their work. As Fred Ross Sr. used to remind his organizers: "People will appreciate what they do for you far more than what you do for them."[32]

GET REAL: DRAFT A MESSAGE COMMUNICATIONS PLAN WITH A BALANCED MEDIA MIX

Bring news to people the way they prefer to receive it, and talk to people the way they talk to one another.

Media Outlets. List the media outlets that cover your community; include their Web sites, contact information, advertising options and rates, and timing of your proposed ads:

Outlets	Contact	Ad Options	Rates	Timing
Newspapers				
Broadcast television				
Local cable				
Community weeklies				
Blogs				
Radio				
Billboards				

Organization or Campaign-Generated Messaging. List the activities that you will undertake to connect with people:

Activity	Message Topic	Budget	Timing
Mail			
Phone banks			
Texting			
Free "earned" media events			
Viral marketing			

Media Monitoring. For each item, list media outlets, contact information; blog the results:

- Action alerts (urging supporters to speak out)
- Success stories (post results of any letters published or calls aired on blog)

SIX

★ ★ ★

Raise the Money

Raise money as fast as you can, hold it as long as you can, and spend it as slowly as you can. —*Campaign adage*

To attract people to your vision and plan, you must be able to ask for money. Most people want to be asked to invest in a cause and will participate if they have a stake in the mission.

Your pitch should include the four campaign metrics: management, message, money, and mobilization.

Management: your solid team of professionals with ethics and experience.

Message: a values-based, authentic message that sets forth your call to service and the vision, ideas, and values that will achieve the vision.

Money: a detailed campaign plan that budgets the resources (that is, how their money will be spent).

Mobilization: the volunteers and voters you are attracting to your mission.

Political fund-raising entails a particular challenge because, unlike charitable donations, donors get no tax benefit for giving. For campaign leaders and candidates, even the healthiest dose of personal ambition is insufficient to sustain the stamina necessary to spend several hours a day "dialing for dollars." You must keep your focus on the larger goals: your vision, ideas, and values.

UNDERSTAND THE WHY OF FUND-RAISING

The most fundamental lesson in political fund-raising is understanding why people give. Most people give because they understand that money is necessary to win a campaign and achieve a vision, and they want to participate in an effort to create the kind of future they want to see for themselves, their families, their communities, and their society.

The late Ann Richards, former governor of Texas, provided this plainspoken advice at a women's networking lunch I attended in the 1990s: "If you were hit by a car and someone opened your purse to find identification, and they looked at your checkbook, what would they see? How would your expenses and priorities identify you?" Many people tithe to charity or to their church or synagogue. Others set aside a certain amount of money each year for political giving. If you were to think about the money you spend on your ideals, and what motivates you to do so, you can get a sense of what inspires other people. As Governor Richards said, it's all right there in the checkbook.

You must view any potential donor through the prism of why they are giving. Do they know you well? Do they work in the same profession as you do? Do they believe in your values? Do they disagree with your opponent's values? Do they think you are going to win and want to invest in your leadership?

Until you know what motivates potential donors, you cannot successfully attract their support. How will you know? Start with people you already know and who know you; then grow your campaign from there. Your campaign leadership teams will develop information as the campaign goes along, and your outreach will adapt to include whatever you learn about people as you meet them and they interact with your campaign.

Once you know why people give, you can tailor your requests to their needs and interests.

If you know that potential donors care about the environment and your "ask" is to raise funds for a conservancy, point out the good work they have already done for the cause, your plan to spend this money effectively to preserve natural resources, the need to act quickly, and the integrity with which the campaign is being waged.

If you know that potential donors want to elect women to office and you are calling about an event for women leaders who support a female candidate, you can discuss the vision of equal partnership in politics and government and the great ideas and ideals this woman brings to the table. You can also mention the women's networks that are participating in the campaign or the event.

Apply your research wisely by appealing to the reason donors give so that with every call you are making a personal connection between your vision and the donor's vision.

BE WILLING TO ASK FOR MONEY

You have heard your call to service, you work hard with your management team, you believe in your message, and you have a great plan to mobilize support. All you need is money to make it happen.

Some people are reluctant to ask for money. Dotty LeMieux says that people new to campaigns, particularly novice candidates, "shy away from fund-raising, feeling that it would make them appear too 'slick' and detract from their grassroots approach."[1]

She advises people to realize that as Jesse Unruh, the former California State treasurer, famously said, Money is the Mother's Milk of Politics: "They need to learn that money is a necessary evil to get their message out to the voters. They don't have to have the most money, but they do need enough to be viable."[2]

Environmental advocate and Democratic National Committeewoman Rachel Binah says that asking for money for yourself is "a measure of what you think of yourself."[3]

Binah offers this advice for aspiring public servants: be a giver. "You can't ask for money, comfortably, unless you give yourself. Think of the money you give to charities and campaigns. What motivates you? Think of other people the same way—you just have to look beneath the surface."

"Ask people, even if you don't think they have money," Binah advises. She recalls raising money for a Women Making History lunch supporting Barbara Boxer's first Senate campaign. "It cost $150 to attend, and it was in San Francisco, which meant that we, in Mendocino, would have to travel several hours in each direction to go to it. I asked everyone I could think of to come to the luncheon, and a woman heard about it and was upset that I hadn't asked her. She was a woman who was poor, I thought. But her mother had died and left her some money, and she wanted to spend it on Barbara Boxer. This woman continued to donate money for each campaign thereafter."

Finally, Binah urges, "Ask people who are always asked. They are the ones who always give. Don't let them off the hook because you want to protect them. Don't say to yourself, 'Oh, I can't ask them, because they're always asked, and they always donate to everything.' That's what you want!"[4]

MAP OUT YOUR
CAMPAIGN FUND-RAISING PLAN

You must start with a clear idea of how much you can raise for a campaign. Knowing that amount is an important test of your viability as a candidate. If you cannot raise enough money to win, you should not run. On the other hand, if you can raise the money, you should put together a detailed plan of where your money will come from and how you plan to bring it in. That is your finance plan.

Good campaign fund-raising is really about organization and discipline. It should start in the beginning of your campaign with a comprehensive finance plan. The following are seven elements to a good campaign finance plan:

1. *Forecast how much money you will need to win.* You have the campaign budget, developed by the finance council, that lays out the dollar amounts and percentages to be spent on the management, message, money, and mobilization needed to win. Consider what past campaigns have raised for this position. Using these figures as a guideline, start setting some goals. Are you in the ballpark? Make sure you plan to get the money in by the time you want to spend it. If you want to be on TV in August, you had better have a plan to raise the necessary money.

2. *Establish control mechanisms.* Check with an attorney so that you know who can give how much money to your race. There may be individual and PAC donation limits for a primary and general election, or overall limits

on local, state, or federal giving. Also, decide whether
there are sources of funds you will avoid. Some candidates decide early on that they will not take money from
certain industries (such as tobacco) or from special interest groups. Draw ethical lines, and figure out other
sources to get the funds needed. Establish management
and internal controls so that you are prepared to vet and
process all potential donations to be sure they comply
with the legal and ethical lines you have drawn. These
controls will facilitate your ongoing fund-raising efforts
as well as your campaign finance reporting. Purchase the
software needed to track past and potential contributors
and to prepare campaign finance filing reports.

3. *Decide if your campaign is willing to borrow money.* It
   is always better to think through these options at the
   start of a campaign than it is to wait until the very end.
   The question of going into debt is a personal one for
   candidates and family: Are you willing to borrow
   money? Can you give yourself a loan? Is your call to
   service such that you would sacrifice retirement dreams
   or mortgage your house for the opportunity to achieve
   your vision?

4. *Identify your prospective donors.* Consider people who
   know you. Have you given any money to their organizations or charities? Do you have a personal Rolodex or
   holiday card list of family and friends? Start with their
   names and affiliations. Then branch out to your community inventory (see chapter 2, Know Your Community),
   and prepare a list of people you know from those political
   and social networks. A review of annual reports from
   local cultural institutions, civic organizations, and nonprofits may help you become familiar with the commu-

nity's philanthropists. Have you helped them in their
fund-raising? If so, they might be inclined to support
you in your efforts. Find people who disagree with your
opponent's views. If you are running against someone
who consistently votes with an industry, for example,
consider the organizations that oppose special treatment
for that industry. Also consider people who tend to contribute to candidates for office. There are many Internet
sites, starting with the Federal Election Commission
(FEC; www.fec.gov), that have donor lists. These lists
include the donor's name, contribution amount, occupa-
tion, employer, and address. FEC lists are available to the
public and are often available online. Most state and local
election offices also maintain lists of political donors.

Ethics are important here: although it is legal to look
up the history of political contributions made by individuals, please note that FEC information is available for research purposes only—to determine a donor's ability to
give—not for fund-raising. The ideal fund-raising path is
to ask prominent people who support you to write a letter or solicitation to their supporters recommending you
as a candidate.

As with all venues of the campaign, you must not seek
support in a vacuum. Peer-to-peer networking is essential
to fund-raising. Although you must make a personal appeal, you must also reinforce your "ask" with a prospective donor's peer in your campaign—your family, staff,
or leadership team (kitchen cabinet, house meeting hosts,
finance council, volunteer corps, or election protection
team).

5. *Identify your available tools.* There are a variety of fund-
raising tools needed to raise funds; you must outline each

of them, including candidate call time, personal meetings and events, phone banks, direct mail, and e-mail.

6. **Match up donors with tools and targeted dollars.** Review your prospective donors and think about the best way to approach the sources on your list. The best way may be holding a reception or just a simple phone call. If possible, raising money over the phone is always the best way because you do not incur overhead costs associated with fund-raising events. Then chart out the donors, the tools, and the targeted dollars to be raised.

7. **Prepare a fund-raising kit for potential donors.** Your kit should include a résumé or candidate biography that includes a clear explanation of your call to service, vision for the future, big ideas, and values to achieve the vision. You also need a copy of the campaign plan, the fund-raising plan, and any recent polling or articles about the race, as well as a list of your endorsements, some campaign literature, and photographs. If you are working with a nonprofit, profiles on the people you help and testimonials are important. If you are working with a candidate, provide a candidate's photo so people can see whom they are supporting.

Encourage potential donors to follow their money. Making sure your Web site is updated with volunteer and service activities, identify where donations will be reported: political campaigns file with elections boards, and nonprofits file with the Internal Revenue Service. If you are working with a nonprofit or a campaign in which a nonprofit is taking the lead, the organization's filings show how resources are raised and spent. For example, if you are raising funds for a ballot initiative spearheaded by a local business group, invite potential donors to look at the campaign's and the group's financial filings to see how they raise and spend their money and what coalition networks they form with other community organizations.

EMPOWER YOUR DONORS TO INVEST IN YOUR VISION AND PLAN

Many people find that the most difficult part of any public service enterprise is asking for money to help achieve its vision. "The key is donor's choice," says Brian Wolff, executive director of the Democratic Congressional Campaign Committee with over a dozen years experience in national fundraising for campaigns ranging from Congress to the presidency. Wolff advises: "If donors feel empowered by the information you give them about your candidacy or cause, they usually become investors."[5]

Wolff offers five elements to consider when asking for money.

1. Asking for support and receiving it is the single most important indicator in a campaign—it shows that people believe in you and are willing to invest in your cause/campaign.

2. Use the power of information. Keeping your investors (donors) informed is hugely important. It's just as important if they haven't contributed to you or have declined to support you. Progress reports on your campaign are important to those that support you and those yet to support you. You never know when something on your report will spur them to action. Also, it shows them that you are willing to work for their support and you will earn it.

3. Your donors are intellectual resources, not just bank accounts. Look to this base of support for ideas when you factor in their expertise on the issues.

4. Activate your friends and family network. Friends and family are the single most important group that you can activate for your candidacy as third-party validators—they can increase your universe and network by reaching out as real ambassadors for your campaign.

5. Stay personal—the more personal you can keep your communications the better. YOU should be the voice on the phone they hear first—not an assistant. It shows that you respect them and that you take responsibility for making "the ask" of them directly. In these days of the Internet and real-time technology, the art of the handwritten note never goes unnoticed.[6]

VARY YOUR FUND-RAISING TOOLS

Dialing for dollars. Before you start, have your fund-raising kit ready with any up-to-date news, polling or literature, and call sheets, and have water and snacks and a good assistant ready to help you keep the calls moving. For inspiration you may want to have photographs of the people being helped by your nonprofit or cause. Candidates may want a family photo and pictures of people you have met on the campaign trail whom you are seeking the opportunity to serve.

To make personal calls to potential givers, you will want to have "call sheets" with the names of potential donors at the start of each day. These are not names taken out of the phone book; they are people who are accustomed to giving money to politicians, and some of them like doing it. Their personal and giving information should be on the call sheet for reference in the conversation.

To appreciate the craft of personal fund-raising for candidates, acknowledge that unless and until we have publicly financed campaigns, any candidate must make a commitment to spend several hours a day on the phone. Knowing that it must be done—and that most donors know that too—will help you call.

Ideally, potential givers will have been called by someone on the campaign to make sure they are in the office that day. They will also have received information, either by fax or by e-mail. You then call potential donors and ask for a *specific* contribution. If you ask for support, the person may say yes and send you a check for $25. If you want $500, then you must ask for it. The best way to do this is to tell the person that you are preparing your budget for mailing and you need to know if you can count on $500 from them. Then *pause.* Anticipate silence—do not rush to fill it. Too many people rush to fill a silence, usually by lowering the amount requested. Don't do that. Drink your water if necessary. Let your request stand for itself, and respect the donor's need to think about your request and commit.

Receiving a contribution is always a great feeling. "It's like getting a scholarship," says Brian Wolff. "It's literally like someone believes that you have a future and is investing in you."[7] Savor the moment—put the name on a donor's chart, let yourself have a treat or a quick high five—before you get on with the next call.

One way to keep your spirits up while you call is to intersperse calls to people who you know are more likely to give with other less likely donors so that after a certain point you get a reward of a talk with a good friend or true believer.

If you get a large commitment, you may also be able to sway other callers, not just with a positive attitude but with specific inspiration to join in a success. For example: "Ms. X just gave us $500 to help with the printing of the mailer; now we need you to invest in the stamps."

Once you get a commitment, that conversation is followed by a letter thanking the contributor for their promise to provide $500 for the cause. If the person requests additional information, fax them immediately, and place their call sheet in a stack to be re-called the following day.

People who have already given some money should be called and asked for more, depending on how much you believe they are capable of giving. If they say they cannot give any more, they should be asked to host a meeting or for the names of five people who may contribute.

The most common problems with call time are the ones created by callers themselves. Callers sometimes decline to ask for specific amounts, are not firm with people who have pledged to contribute, and do not set aside enough time to make their calls. Avoid these problems by giving callers the support and practice that they need to succeed. Find the right person to put in the room to support the caller. Celebrate successes. Keep the right snack food within reach. These small things will make the operation run smoothly. Remember: every donor appreciates your thanks. Make thank-yous a priority!

Meetings and events. Sometimes a personal meeting will be necessary to secure an individual contribution. Using the same techniques as during call time, be sure to have updated information in your fund-raising kit, be fully educated about the donor's political and giving history, ask for a specific amount, respect the pause—drink that water if you must to stop yourself from answering your own question or lowering your request—and, as always, listen and say thank-you.

Events are wonderful opportunities to bring people together to see the candidate, get a campaign update, and invest in the values, ideas, and vision of the campaign. They can also be expensive unless you plan wisely. Some campaigns use the house meeting model as a small-donor fund-raising vehicle. For example, Congressman Chris Murphy of Connecticut had over sixty house parties at which he recruited campaign donors and volunteers. All attendees were invited to attend for free; upon hearing the message, some wrote checks, some enlisted as volunteers, and still others opted to host future events. By giving people the opportunity to "kick the tires" on his campaign up close, Murphy was able to expand his network and attract the support—and dollars—necessary to win.[8]

Phone banks. Setting up a phone bank to follow up on mailed invitations is a good way to increase event attendance. A call reminds prospects about the event and greatly increases the likelihood that they will buy a ticket and attend. Also, if prospects say they cannot attend an event, they can still be asked for a contribution. Phone banks can also be used to collect on pledges following phone solicitations. Once a donor has made a pledge on the phone, be sure the campaign sends a confirmation letter stating the exact amount of the pledge. Phone calls should follow the letters to remind donors of their commitments. Similarly, phone banks can be used to collect money that was promised but did not materialize at an event.

Direct mail solicitation. "Direct mail" describes two types of fund-raising done through the mail. The lowest-risk form of direct mail fund-raising is the resolicitation of your campaign's donor file. Experts estimate that donor resolicitation will provide close to 80 percent of the net income from direct mail. At the other end of the spectrum, direct mail also means cold prospecting for new donors—an operation that is considered successful if it just breaks even. The goal of cold prospecting is to acquire new donors who are then resolicited several times for additional contributions.

Before embarking on an expensive and high-risk prospecting venture, consider whether the campaign has the expertise in-house to run a prospecting program; whether the campaign can afford to hire a mail consultant; whether there is a large enough potential universe of prospects who would be interested in the campaign to make a professional prospecting program economical in the short-term and profitable in the long-term; and whether the campaign has time to implement a successful direct-mail program.

Logistically, your next step is production and printing: prepare the letter, envelope, and business reply envelope so that they are ready for the printer; decide how the campaign will mail the solicitation (through volunteers or a mail shop); and identify a good union printer that can meet the campaign's deadlines and give a good price. Once you are set to go, have several people proofread the copy to avoid embarrassing errors.

Proofread your mailer one more time after you print. It is better (though highly regrettable) to lose money than your reputation. A candidate for state attorney general once printed up thousands of postcards for voters introducing himself as a "compatet" attorney. Luckily, he had a *competent* staffer who caught the error, and his team spent the day shredding, instead of stamping, the doomed mailers.

Make sure the basic facts about each piece of mail are recorded accurately so the campaign can evaluate the results. A tracking system should include the date mailed, package code (if different packages are sent to the same list), number of pieces mailed, number of contributors, daily and running totals), the total amount contributed (daily and running totals), percentage return (number of contributors divided by number mailed), average contribution, dollar return per thousand mailed, and cost of mailing per thousand mailed. This data will allow comparison between the results of different prospect mailings to determine which lists were successful.

You've got e-mail: online fund-raising. Communicating online is the wave of the future. Low administrative costs can yield high returns if you plan correctly. A credit card donation means a sure thing, so make sure you can take credit card payments online. You can purchase software from your Web designer or the bank handling your campaign account. Remember the campaign's Internet protocols, and be sure that your donation lists are used for campaign and reporting use only, and that your Web systems are free of spyware and viruses.

If your fund-raising plea is going out to an online network, remember that friend-raising comes before fund-raising. Be mindful of Tim Tagaris's "ATM pin number": "direct communication with online communities, involving netroots in your campaign, outreach to opinion leaders, and your stand on the issues."[9]

Remember, your fund-raising request is subject to the same campaign protocols as every other communication. Potential supporters, as well as reporters and your opposition, are receiving these e-mails. The rules of netiquette all

ONLINE FUND-RAISING

1. **Present your vision** to your audience. You will be e-mailing to supporters who will be asked to forward your message on to their friends and family, so speak in your own voice, communicate with simplicity, and provide links for helpful information. Your credibility is key, so if you are describing your stance or an opponent's stance on an issue as a means of gaining support, be sure to be accurate and post to a trusted Web resource for verification.

2. **Send** to an audience you already know is supportive of your candidacy. If you are just growing your list, do not start by asking for money—join with a third-party validator and circulate your message to their list. For example, former Senator Max Cleland, a hero of the Vietnam War, sent an e-mail to veterans and military families across the country entitled "Send a Marine to Congress." That summer 2005 e-mail helped raise the national profile—and the campaign coffers—of candidate Paul Hackett in Ohio's Second Congressional District among those who knew of and trusted Senator Cleland.

3. **Describe** in precise detail the value of the contribution. For example, a $10,000 goal seems like a vast sum of money going into the nowhere land of a campaign treasury. But $10,000 that represents 100 rental vans for get-out-the-vote, 1,000 volunteer meals, 2,500 signs, or 5,000 bumper stickers is a defined precise goal.

(continued)

ONLINE FUND-RAISING
(continued)

4. **Encourage** your supporters by showcasing their success. Fill a thermometer, a baseball bat (popularized by Governor Howard Dean), or some other graphic so people can literally see their money in action online. Clever graphics that relate to your candidate are always a plus.

5. **Track** your readers and responses. A good e-mail vendor will have statistics on when people tend to open mail and how many open yours, click on your links, or give through a solicitation. This accounting is crucial in determining your success.

6. **Innovate** so that your readers will want to open your e-mails. Be creative in asking for action items—for example, signing a petition, contributing for a specific campaign event, blanketing a community with signs, or hosting a house meeting on a given night.

7. **Format** for success. Most requests follow this pattern:
   Dear First Name -
   Two paragraphs
   http:// Link to action on Web site
   Two paragraphs
   http:// Link to same action on Web site
   Two paragraphs
   Closing
   Signed, (name)
   P.S.
   http:// Link to same action on Web site

apply, so don't say anything online that the campaign would not authorize you to say off-line and in person.

FINANCE REPORTING

Your finance reports are legal documents. Treat them with care. Do not file false, incomplete, or controversial finance reports. Get an attorney involved early in the process to make sure that you meet all the public requirements. Find someone you trust to act as treasurer of the campaign with responsibility for filing all the campaign finance reports required under city, county, state, and federal laws. In addition to your treasurer, someone with trusted judgment should review your finance reports before they are filed. This person should check to make sure that you have not accepted money from a disreputable individual or organization.

If you are working with a candidate or cause that is filing campaign finance reports, the press will be looking at your quarterly reports to see what shape you are in. If you are working on a ballot initiative, be sure that your fund-raising matches your message. For example, if you are raising funds to effect change in a community, your donors should mostly live in that community. If it is a poor community, what you lack in the size of contributions you might make up for in the number of donors.

If you are running for office yourself, it is especially important to show wide diversity in the source of your contributions. You never want the public to think you are being underwritten by lobbyists or people outside the community you seek to represent. Again, your report is an expression of your message: if you are a homegrown campaign, the number or percentage of local donors is key. If you are trying to create an aura of invincibility, the sheer money figures may be what you highlight. Whatever your message, have your numbers ready to tell the story of your campaign in terms of total donations, average donations, Internet-based donations, and local donations.

Compliance with the elections regulations is extremely important. Confusion over intricacies of the laws and filing mistakes can lead to embarrassing fines, negative press coverage, and an issue your opponent can attack.

Best practices for filing your reports includes the following: get a lawyer, get all advice in writing, know the regulations and filing deadlines, procure computer software that enables you to produce reports quickly and accurately, entrust at least one person with the responsibility of making sure you remain in full compliance with the law, and be sure to check the relevant government Web sites regularly for updates.

The run-up to any filing deadline adds pressure. Don't let the deadline change your campaign policy or your management and internal controls (for example, be sure to keep any no-tobacco or no–special interest pledges you may have made). Be aware that watchdogs actually score political action committees on whether they file donor information accurately.

Finally, vet and research any contributions well before the deadline. No one reads your campaign filings more closely than your opponent!

★ ★ ★

GET REAL: PREPARE A FUND-RAISING PLAN

1. Establish Budget Goals, Controls, and Plans

- Forecast the budget, starting with what past campaigns have raised for this cause.

- Check with an attorney so that you know who can give how much money.
- Decide what kind of money you will raise and from whom. Are there sources of funds you will avoid?
- Establish management and internal controls to vet and process all potential donations to facilitate your ongoing fund-raising efforts as well as your campaign finance reporting.
- Map out your campaign plan and projected dollars (and percentages) to be spent on the management, message, money, and mobilization needed to win.

2. Identify Your Prospective Donors

- You: Are you willing to borrow money? Can you give yourself a loan? Would you mortgage your house in order to win?
- List your family and friends.
- List your peers: high school, college or professional school graduates; co-workers from any jobs or volunteer positions held; people to whom you have donated political or charitable contributions.
- Consider your opponent's record and any political antagonists who might fund you.
- Consider people who tend to give to elected officials. Will any current or former officeholders contact their networks for you?

3. Identify Your Available Tools

- Candidate Call Time
- Phone Banks
- Personal Meetings and Events

- Direct Mail
- E-mail

4. Match Up Donors with Tools and Targeted Dollars

Review your prospective donors and think about the best way to approach the sources on your list. Then chart out the donors, the tools, and the targeted dollars to be raised:

Donors	Tools	Targeted Dollars
You	Bank Loan	
Family	Call/Meetings/Events	
Friends	Call/Meeting/Events/ E-mail	
School Alums	Phone Banks/Meetings	
Peers	Events/Direct Mail/ E-mail	
Community Leaders	Call Time/Meetings/ Events/E-mail	
People You Have Supported	Call Time/Meetings/ Events/E-mail	

SEVEN

Mobilize to Win

Whoever owns the ground wins the election.
—*House Speaker Nancy Pelosi*

Whether you are running for president of the PTA or the United States, the team with the best volunteer operation will bring out the most voters on Election Day.

How will you do this? You go to each and every person who was a part of anything you have ever done in public life and recruit them to help you bring home the votes on Election Day. Some volunteers will have been with you from day one. Others may have put up a sign or written a check or attended an event. Still others may be friends or colleagues of people who support you, your cause, or your candidate.

RECRUIT YOUR VOLUNTEER CORPS

Public service takes people. A passionate, engaged volunteer workforce can make your offices or campaign headquarters hum with excitement. That kind of energy welcomes people to your effort and encourages them to participate.

When volunteers enter a vibrant campaign headquarters, they are likely to see a scene such as this: One group of volunteers is preparing targeting maps for the distribution of door-hangers to voters who have received mail from the campaign and visits from precinct walkers. In another area, phone-bankers are calling absentee voters. While most callers are leaving messages on voicemail services, one woman strikes gold: a live person telling her there are five "yes" votes in one household. The group cheers, then returns to work. Another group waving scanners, which look like electric razors attached to power cords, over papers with bar codes to capture the phone bank results in yes/no/undecided/absentee categories. Ironing boards that have been used to register voters are stacked neatly under a wall of fame with names and photos of outstanding volunteers. Signs around the headquarters read "50 percent plus your vote to win."

Understand why people volunteer. People volunteer on campaigns for a number of reasons: to be part of a network of people who share their values, to promote a particular candidate or cause, or to gain recognition and respect in the community. Nearly all share the goal of making the future better. Chris Finnie, a Democracy for America volunteer, expressed it this way: "After a Meetup, a woman stopped and asked me why I spent all the time and money I do on political activism. I told her I have a grown son. She said she did too. So I asked her if, when she had children, she didn't feel that she had given them a gift—a gift of life. She said yes. I then asked her if this was what she had in mind. She said no. I said me either, and that's why I do what I do—so I can leave my son the sort of world I promised him."[1]

Find volunteers by activating your networks. The technology, coalition, and human networks that Lezlee Westine described are the prime sources for your volunteer corps. You identified your networks in the public service fitness exercise. You inventoried peer-to-peer networks and cross-checked to see who among your networks was active in others in the know-your-community exercise. You drew from your networks to develop management, message, money, and mobilization expertise in the build-your-leadership-teams exercise. You built your message with the help of experts and allies from your networks in the define-your-message exercise. Now it is time to bring everyone together in your volunteer corps.

Recruiting volunteers from your networks will provide a cadre of campaign ambassadors to represent your cause or candidate. If you are working with a candidate, be sure to draw from people who have worked directly with that person. Two former teachers, Mike Honda and Tim Walz, attracted former students and parents from their teaching days to their campaigns when they ran for Congress.

Congressman Mike Honda, a former teacher and principal from the San Jose area, was attacked in his 2000 run for Congress with a hit piece called "Honda's Criminal Record." In fact, Honda's only brush with the law was as an infant, when he and his Japanese American parents were placed in a World War II internment camp. Honda counterpunched with testimonials from his network of former students and parents. When I volunteered on the phone banks, one of our favorite stories was of an elderly woman who called and said that she read about Honda's criminal record but then heard about his teaching and concluded that she was glad he had turned his life around and become a productive member of society.

Congressman Tim Walz, a former high school teacher and longtime Minnesota National Guardsman, earned the support of students he had taught and coached as well as of those with whom he had served in the reserves. When I traveled to Minnesota in the summer of 2006, many Walz enthusiasts commented that his former students were integral to his volunteer corps because they could effectively validate his views on education and the war during his 2006 run for office, giving voters a sense of his character and a reason to trust him.

To activate your networks, start the way Honda and Walz did, by contacting your friends and colleagues and getting them involved. Look for a leader who can keep track of other volunteers and start scheduling regular volunteer activities. The best way to find new volunteers is to build on your existing base. Have your volunteers hold house meetings to bring their own friends into contact with the campaign. Every person who attends the first meeting should be asked to come to the next meeting with five friends. Then make the same request at the next meeting, and in this way start to build a core group of hundreds of supporters.

One way to find new volunteers is to approach existing organizations that are supporting your cause or candidate. Ask them to send people over to help with a specific project— knocking on doors or putting together a mailing. These people can help find other members of their organization who are willing to get involved in your campaign on an individual basis.

If you are working with a political campaign, make sure that everyone on your team carries volunteer sign-up cards with them at all times. Everyone the team members meet who says they would like to volunteer should be asked to fill out a card and then be called to get them involved.

Another approach to recruiting volunteers is to reach out to young people and empower them to get involved at all levels of your public service effort. Arab American Institute

CALL TO SERVICE
JAMES ZOGBY

James Zogby, executive director of the Arab American Institute, traces his call to service to the strong influence of his mother, who urged her children to get involved in community affairs. "After receiving the benefit of a Jesuit education, I was challenged by my mother's injunction into civil rights and peace work," recalls Zogby. "Later in my life, I took a long, hard look at the needs of my community, especially the most recent immigrants, and saw that as a challenge to service. My work in founding civic education projects to organize Arab Americans to vote and become involved in U.S. politics are but extensions of the early influences that motivated me toward service. Nothing gives me more pride today than to see immigrants become citizens and register to vote for the first time, and to see their children involved in our many internship programs, working in politics, civil rights, government institutions, and other forms of community service."

Source: James Zogby, e-mail, May 2007.

founder James Zogby says: "It's like *Field of Dreams*—'if you build it, they will come.'" Zogby has issued calls for service in activities including voter registration, volunteering at events, participation in community cleanup days, and internships in Washington, D.C. "Young people want to serve. All you need to do is ask them and provide them with the opportunity."[2]

KEEP YOUR VOLUNTEERS

Almost as important as finding volunteers is keeping the ones you have.

Start by making new volunteers feel welcome. Every volunteer who joins the effort should have training and orientation. As mentioned in chapter 3, Build Your Leadership Teams, the volunteer coordinator should interview new recruits to match their skills and networks to the needs of the campaign and should train these new ambassadors with campaign protocols. Volunteers should know the major issues or controversies of the campaign and what ads each campaign is running on TV, radio, and/or the Internet. If volunteers are working for an initiative, they should know what it would do to change the law and how voters can get more information if they want it. Volunteers should have a solid understanding of the task they are performing, the issues they are talking about, and how their efforts fit into the big picture and campaign plan.

If you are working with new volunteers, take ten or fifteen minutes to talk and make sure people are confident in what they are doing. Pair them up with campaign staff or an experienced and trusted volunteer to make a few calls or knock on a few doors together before you put them out on their own. Making sure they are confident and comfortable in what they are doing will not only keep them coming back but will make them effective representatives of the campaign.

Give volunteers meaningful work. People who take time out of their own lives to help with the campaign expect to work when they arrive. Always make sure that you have a stack of work for volunteers to do at the office. If someone shows up ready to knock on doors, get that person some materials and get them out into the community. If volunteers feel that you do not need them, they will not come back. On the other hand, if they believe that there is always important work to do, they will start showing up regularly at the office.

Volunteer coordinators should try to set regular schedules for all the volunteers. Having regular times allows the campaign to schedule work to fulfill the service mission and tasks. Also, volunteers will come to think of the campaign as a regular part of their week. For example, Wednesdays will become their day to go help out at the campaign office.

Appreciate that volunteers don't come free. In addition to regularly thanking volunteers for their work and giving them tasks that make them feel important, there are a few other things you can do to keep them happy. Offer transportation if necessary. If someone stays at the office late, offer to coordinate carpools for rides home. Always provide your volunteers with food and refreshments. Make sure that the campaign leaders regularly take time to drop by the campaign office during the phone bank or precinct walk in order to talk with volunteers and thank them for their time. This show of appreciation is essential for candidates. Have events once a week after precinct walks to give volunteers an opportunity to meet other volunteers and campaign staff.

Feed your volunteers. It is said that an army marches on its stomach. The same is true for your volunteer army. Alec Bash and the DemocracyAction network in San Francisco fed volunteers well, setting up phone banks at people's homes with coffee and bagels for people who came to call for over a dozen candidates in swing districts during 2006. The volunteer appreciation parties were sources of great food, lively conversation, and, of course, more recruitment.[3]

Thank your volunteers. Keep your regular volunteers updated on the campaign, and let them know their contribution is making a difference. For example: "Thanks to your efforts on the phones last week, we've identified three hundred new supporters. We're right on track to reach our goals." Thom O'Shaughnessy, who was active with Veterans for Kerry in 2004 and now serves with the Los Angeles–area SoCal Grassroots network, says that "volunteer recognition is vital." In 2006, the SoCal Grassroots network made campaign sun visors for people who walked three times and personalized sweatshirts for "Team Ann Richards"—the cadre of people who walked weekend after weekend throughout the fall, dedicating their service to the late Texas governor. "These are some of my most treasured campaign items that I have received over all my years of field work," he says.[4]

Thank-you letters, walls of fame, voter contact charts, and other forms of public recognition in your headquarters and on your Web site let volunteers know how much you value them. Comedy shows, music, and visits from all-stars are also great ways to thank volunteers and keep them engaged. Giving respect and recognition to people who help out because your campaign is part of their call to service is essential to the success of your shared mission.

Avoid behavior that could lead to embarrassment. Beware of engaging in illegal or provocative behavior. Many a campaign has been forced to apologize when people were arrested for stealing or defacing signs. You never want to send your candidate on television to explain that your campaign was indeed responsible for some embarrassing act. The opposition is working hard enough to cause you problems, so there is no reason to cause your own.

Promote effective controversy. Mobilizing sometimes means controversy. For example, Neighbor to Neighbor launched the International Boycott of Salvadoran Coffee and Folgers in December 1989, just five days after the Salvadoran military's brutal assassination of six Jesuits, their housekeeper, and her daughter. Neighbor to Neighbor's boycott strategy to build real economic pressure for a negotiated peace settlement was organized with International Longshoreman Workers Union (ILWU) president James "Jimmy" Herman. They sealed off the West Coast from shipments of Salvadoran coffee for two years and pressured three multinational corporations, which represented $70 billion of annual revenue, to push the Salvadoran government and Salvadoran coffee industry to negotiate a peace settlement. "We had learned from Cesar Chavez to be direct, forceful and confrontational when necessary to really speak truth to power," says Fred Ross. "The Coffee Boycott was successful because people's moral outrage was effectively focused on an essential economic target that put real pressure on the Salvadoran government to negotiate a peace settlement."[5]

Track your volunteers. Maintain an electronic, regularly updated database of everyone who has volunteered or expressed an interest in volunteering on your campaign. Back up your database on a CD or other portable storage medium. Whenever possible, choose one person (your volunteer coordinator) to invite volunteers back to the campaign so they can start building a personal relationship with the campaign.

TALK TO PEOPLE

The best way to persuade people to support your cause is to talk to them.

Peer-to-peer outreach. Many of the networks get involved and turn out their own members for a cause or candidate. In 2006 Democratic challengers established Vets to Vets phone banks specifically aimed at fostering dialogue between and among veterans and military families. Specialty phone banks were created when campaigns secured the list of Veterans Affairs (VA) recipients in their communities and cross-checked that against voter files, adding a new layer to get-out-the-vote efforts across America.

Knock on every door. When you work on a campaign, be prepared to reach out to everyone regardless of political party. This is crucial in swing districts where people historically split their ticket between Democrats and Republicans, or in districts where there is no clean partisan or ideological majority.

For instance, Colorado's Seventh Congressional District is one of the most evenly split congressional district in the country, with equal parts Republican, Democratic, and unaffiliated voters. A Republican won the seat by only 121 votes in 2002. Two years later, John Kerry won the district in the presidential race. Ed Perlmutter, a former Colorado state senator whose interest in politics bloomed early as a boy helping his father canvass local neighborhoods for various campaigns, was determined to talk to as many people as he could. He spent months knocking on thousands of doors and speaking to Democrats, Republicans, and Independents about the war, the economy, and health care. Stem cell research was a significant personal issue: one reason he ran for Congress was to push for expanded research, which could help cure his oldest daughter, who has epilepsy. All three of his daughters volunteered on the campaign and starred in his TV commercials. After over a year of walking door to door to door,

Perlmutter was able to build a commanding lead, attract a large volunteer corps, and win the election.[6]

SHOE LEATHER POLITICS: WALK THOSE PRECINCTS

Best practices for making house calls. A few tips for volunteers before you go knocking on doors.

First, think locally: when you go into a community, remember politics, sports, and revenge. Politics: if a particular elected official is popular and you are talking to her voters, name drop if she supports your candidate or cause, and don't insult her if she does not. Sports: some communities rally around athletic teams, and games are often played on weekends. Find out when the Big Game is, and don't walk or call then. In the special election of 2004 in Kentucky when Ben Chandler was elected to Congress, the Kentucky Wildcats football team was playing the Georgia Bulldogs the Saturday before the election. Precinct walkers for both Chandler and his opponent took an extended break between noon and 3 p.m., resuming our work when the game ended. Revenge: if you are working for a ballot initiative that has been before the voters before, or are canvassing for a candidate in a rematch against someone who defeated them before, remember to show growth and not a grudge by keeping your approach oriented toward the future.

Second, act locally. What you say and do matters. Be polite and respect people. Your appearance matters, so dress comfortably and neatly. "The nose ring belongs on the bull in the field not on the volunteer on the porch," advises national field strategist Donnie Fowler.[7] Be aware of the practices of

BURNS STRIDER:
BIG DADDY'S RULES OF THE ROAD

Before you get out and campaign, consider these words of wisdom from Burns Strider, a Democratic strategist with Capitol Hill experience in outreach to veterans, evangelical Christians, and rural areas. In late 2006 Strider joined Hillary Clinton's presidential campaign.

Most of the campaign rules I follow came from my father. He was known as Big Daddy by nearly everyone in Mississippi. He stood at 6'7"; weighed in at over 330 pounds; and wore a suit, cowboy hat, and cowboy boots seven days a week. He was sheriff of Grenada County for twenty-four years. With my brother currently in the sheriff's office we're still getting elected. I've spent my entire life going door-to-door asking for votes. By the time I was a teenager I knew everyone in Grenada. I knew who was kin, who had marriage plans. Heck, I knew those getting divorced—and usually why. I learned respect for folks. I learned about listening to people and taking them seriously.

BIG DADDY'S RULES OF THE ROAD

1. **A pickup truck beats a Cadillac every day of the week out here in real America.**

TRANSLATION: Don't get fancy. Don't get fancy with your words, with your plan, or with your attitude. Folks are looking for one of them to lead.

2. **Every tub has got to sit on its own bottom.**

TRANSLATION: In the final analysis, the candidate has to carry the day. The candidate is who the voters want to hear from. Only the candidate can speak for the candidate.

3. **If you're driving down the highway and see a car coming toward you in your lane, then you're going to change lanes.**

TRANSLATION: Don't get in the way of your friends. Stay out of other people's races. Stay in your lane and don't bring undue criticism and opposition by being nosy or getting involved where you shouldn't.

4. If you come up on an old yella mangy dog and that dog is barking the Gospel, then let him bark.

TRANSLATION: Don't you challenge, denigrate, or dismiss the faith of anyone. A person's faith represents the core, the essence of who they are. Its one of their most personal choices. You tear that person down if you tear down their faith. Hell, join them. It can probably do you some good.

5. Be careful what you say about someone; you're probably talking to their cousin.

TRANSLATION: You're probably talking to their cousin.

6. In politics if you take a swing at someone, you better be prepared to take one right back.

TRANSLATION: If you're gonna throw a punch, be ready to take a punch. I actually learned this one from Speaker Nancy Pelosi. Think down the road to where your decisions are taking you.

7. Decide what you're going to do, then say you're going to do it, go do it, and then come back and tell them you did it.

TRANSLATION: It's just not enough to believe it or even do it. This is another important rule from Speaker Pelosi. Politics and people must know where you stand on an issue. They must know your actions. Just doing something without getting the news out is a waste of good time.

8. Our veterans stood up for our nation with their lives. If you can't support veterans in your actions as well as your words then just stay on the damn front porch.

TRANSLATION: Pretty words are just that—pretty words. Saluting our veterans and troops must be based in real policy that will reap earned benefits for our veterans and military families—a new, stronger GI Bill of Rights, the end to the Disabled Veterans Tax, a fully funded VA health care system, and fully providing for the health care of our National Guard and Reservists.

Source: Burns Strider, "Big Daddy's Rules of the Road," *Trail Mix,* October 18, 2006; updated by e-mail, May 29, 2007.

different faith communities: Fridays, Saturdays, Sundays, and Wednesday nights are for worship, so voters could be headed to mosque, temple, church, or prayer night when you come knocking. Be ready to listen because voters may vent, especially if they are Independents or undecideds or people who are subjected to a lot of ads. You are not there to argue with people in their homes but to persuade them through your enthusiasm for a cause and responsiveness to their feedback.

Third, know whom to call when a voter needs to know where to vote, when a voter wants to vote early in person or by absentee ballot, or if a voter talks about possible fraud or abuse of voting rights.

Fourth, keep an open feedback loop so that you can report back to headquarters what is or is not working. Use a message-box worksheet to set forth any new counterarguments coming from the volunteers or voters. If an attack mailer comes out and you can bring it back to the headquarters, the campaign can call in the kitchen cabinet and figure out how to get the truth out and determine the best response.

Set up a canvassing operation. Go first to the areas where you are likely to find supporters. Pick the voters who are persuadable and who vote regularly. Pick the houses that have the largest raw numbers of voters in them. Then send your volunteers out to talk to them. The success of your canvassing program will depend on two things: how early you start and how organized you are. Once the basic research on your community is completed, you should know how many votes you will need to win. For each voter your canvassing program records as a supporter, you are one step closer to this goal.

MAKING HOUSE CALLS:
BEST PRACTICES FOR VOLUNTEERS

Think Locally: When You Go into a Community, Know the Customs

✓ Sports (when is the Big Game? Don't walk or call then!)

✓ Faith (Friday, Shabbos or Sunday service; Wednesday prayer meeting)

✓ Weather (if the voter is in the storm cellar, you should be too!)

✓ Dress for success (appearance matters)

Act Locally: What You Say and Do Matters

✓ Manners: R-E-S-P-E-C-T the voters

✓ Listening: voters may vent! (especially Independents or undecideds)

✓ Talking: practice your script before calling or walking

Look Up: What's on the Air

✓ Know the issues

✓ Know what ads each campaign is running (TV, radio, Internet)

✓ Listen to what people are saying about each campaign

Look Down: Read and Study

✓ Know your candidate

✓ Know the opposition

✓ Know local issues and events

(continued)

MAKING HOUSE CALLS:
BEST PRACTICES FOR VOLUNTEERS
(continued)

Look All Around: What to Know or Whom to Call When:

✓ You encounter reporters

✓ A voter needs to know where to vote

✓ A voter wants to vote early in person or by absentee ballot

✓ A voter talks about possible fraud or abuse of voting rights

Keep an Open Feedback Loop

✓ Volunteers: report back to HQ what is (or is not) working

✓ Campaigns: discuss and message-box volunteer and voter-comments

✓ Remember: A positive attitude is everything!

Precinct captains. One excellent way to ensure that volunteers are well trained and your operation is well organized is to create a precinct captain system. Precinct captains are your most trusted and experienced volunteers who take responsibility for a precinct or geographical area. Precinct captains are well versed in how a canvassing operation works, the campaign's message, and the numerical goals in the particular precinct.

Precinct captains provide the extra training and guidance to volunteers that make them extremely effective. On a day when your campaign has a hundred volunteers, it is nearly impossible to properly train all of them quickly. With precinct captains you can assign a group of volunteers to a captain and direct the captain to provide them with in-depth training.

Precinct captains are in charge of collecting walk sheets and reporting numbers from all the volunteers each time they walk and relaying them to the field manager. Good precinct captains will canvass and phone their precinct several times on their own and will recruit volunteers. In campaigns with limited staff, precinct captain systems provide invaluable levels of organization and ensure quality control in terms of volunteer training and accurate voter assessments.

To the extent possible, you should send the same volunteers to talk to the same voters. Then, on Election Day, send the volunteers to the polling places associated with the neighborhoods they have worked. The goal is make voters feel obligated to keep the promise they made to your canvasser to support your campaign.

Watch out for round numbers. Canvassers are talking to real people, so it is unusual for them to come back with exactly fifty supporters, thirty opposed, and ten undecided.

WORK WITH ALLIES AND COALITIONS

Engage your networks. Each of the technology, coalition, and human networks should be engaged for the effort you identified in your community inventory. In addition, there are networks outside your community of people interested in coming in to help with get-out-the-vote efforts. Of the dozens of such groups, two outstanding volunteer networks during 2006 worked in Connecticut and California.

CANVASSING PROGRAM OVERVIEW

Checklist for launching a canvassing program:

✓ Set vote goals for the campaign.

✓ Identify a means to track voter responses (by computer or poll sheet).

✓ Identify an organized individual to drive the operation forward.

✓ Recruit the requisite number of volunteers—always recruit twice as many volunteers as you need to account for no-shows.

✓ Train your canvassers, and make sure they understand the campaign's message.

✓ Prepare literature (walk-pieces) for canvassers.

✓ Set a regular schedule for canvassing: for example, have your volunteers meet every weekend to go out together and knock on doors.

✓ To prevent fatigue, canvassers must dress warmly in the winter and carry water with them in the summer.

✓ Keep walk kits (described below) readily available in the office for people who want to go canvass.

✓ Insist on regular reporting by everyone in your canvassing program—from volunteers and precinct coordinators to your field director. This is the only way to maintain a sense of accountability among your field workers.

Voter contact goals:

Voter goal:　　　　　10,000 votes needed to win (or whatever your total might be)

Votes to identify:　　20,000 (not everyone gives accurate answers to your volunteers)

Voters to contact:　　34,000 (assume 60 percent of those contacted will support you)

Doors to knock on:　22,000 (assume about 1.5 voters per household)

Size of effort: If the average volunteer does 100 doors per week, and you have 50 reliable volunteers, then you can meet your goal in about a month.

Calendar:

9 weeks before the election: Send volunteers out with materials to persuade voters.

6 weeks before the election: Send volunteers back out to identify supporters.

3 weeks before the election: Send volunteers out one last time to confirm supporters and remind them to vote.

Canvassers should always receive a walk kit that includes:

- Map of the area you are asking them to canvass
- List of the voters in the area
- A sample script—possibly talking points
- Tally sheets to record their results
- Walk-pieces to give voters
- Pen, paper, and a clipboard

Former Congressman Sam Gejdenson, who had represented Connecticut's Second District for twenty years, commended the Hilltop Brigade, a self-described e-mail list of friends and friends of friends interested in national and international affairs. In 2004, they had gone with colleagues from Planned Parenthood as Kerry Travelers to Pennsylvania and Florida. In 2006, they stayed closer to home, recruiting volunteers in Connecticut's two "safe" Democratic congressional districts (represented by Rosa DeLauro who helped develop the effort and John Larson who actively supported it) and put them to work in the other three "battleground" congressional districts. They held house meetings to recruit volunteers, committed hundreds of volunteers to work on each of the five Saturdays before Election Day, and then went door-to-door and made phone calls to voters, helping elect two new members of Congress: Chris Murphy and Joe Courtney.[8]

In California, the SoCal Grassroots and the Take Back Red California volunteer networks adopted the "strike team" term from firefighting. They use a coordinated strike team of a driver and two or three walkers so as to blitz a precinct in a short time for maximum penetration. With one local volunteer who knows the area and the local issues, a team of travelers can be used most effectively. Drivers allow for coverage of relatively few voters, such as on a hill or a cul-de-sac. They drop off the walkers at the top of the hill or center of the cul-de-sac and then wait at the bottom to collect the walkers and continue on. [9]

If you are running for office, include your primary foes in your coalitions. After a primary, it is essential that your team present a united front for the general election. One of my rules for baseball is, "Don't boo the home team." That's what the other side is for.

In politics, this sentiment is memorialized in President

Ronald Reagan's eleventh commandment: "Thou shalt not speak ill of another Republican."[10]

In Montana, Democrats expressed President Reagan's eleventh commandment as "Other people pay the price of our divisions." Brad Martin remembers: "We constantly reminded ourselves that other people paid the price of our divisions. When a poor child did not get health care or a hot meal because we were fighting each other, and losing elections, that child paid the price of our divisions."[11]

Martin recommends building a coalition network including your former foes by giving thanks and reaching out. Give thanks to your supporters. Aside from being good manners, thank-yous are essential to keep people feeling appreciated, informed, and inspired. Reach out to your primary opponents and their supporters. You won. Be gracious. Do your politics well so that your opponents and people who supported them feel welcome and motivated to work with you. I walked precincts once for a candidate who had not cleaned up an internal political fight from years before. It was a real problem with some members of his community who wanted him to reconcile with his foe before they would give this candidate a promotion. He didn't, and they didn't.

PLAN A YOUR FIELD OPERATIONS

When planning an electoral campaign, you must set a strategy to accomplish your goals that answers these questions:

- How will we get the petition signatures needed to get on the ballot?
- Who has custody of the most up-to-date voter file? How do we get it?
- How many new voters do we need to register?

- How will our canvassing program run?
- How many volunteers will we need, and where will they come from?
- How will we chase absentee and vote-by-mail voters?
- How will our phone-banking program function?
- How will our get-out-the-vote programs run?

Goals. There is no cookie-cutter approach to these questions. It is important to approach the field with a clear sense of who your base is and who you need to persuade. Try to imagine these voters. Where do they work, shop, and travel? When are they home? The goal of a field campaign is to consolidate and expand your base. Identify your supporters, stay in contact with them, and get them to the polls on Election Day.

Objectives of a field operation. Design field work to fulfill three objectives: (1) identify the key demographic groups, geographic areas, or specific individuals who are most likely to support the campaign; (2) repetitively deliver the message to key groups, areas, and individuals in an effort to persuade them to support your effort; and (3) get those identified supporters out to vote on Election Day.

A successful field operation brings viability to campaigns and brings thousands of uninvolved people into the political process. A visible campaign becomes part of the message: when a campaign has grassroots support, it demonstrates that the cause has broad and deep consensus in the community or that the candidate is someone who is involved in the community and who cares about people.

Hiring field organizers. Plan to hire field organizers to get people involved with your campaign. The best time to hire field organizers is when the public starts to pay attention and you have a reasonable chance of successfully mobilizing people. This timing will depend on your polling and experience.

Opening field offices. Opening field offices turns out to be largely a question of respect in the minds of many of your workers and volunteers. If you do not have a field office in the western part of your community, you must not care about the people who live there—or so the logic goes. Draw on your house meeting hosts to use people's homes for neighborhood headquarters sites. The purpose of a good field office or neighborhood headquarters is to hold literature, give volunteers a place to meet, and give workers a place to make phone calls.

Field tools: You will want to have signs, literature, campaign fashion, creative outreach (see the sidebox), and bilingual materials.

- **Signs.** There are two times when campaign signs matter—at the beginning and on Election Day. In the beginning it is important to show strength. On Election Day, a few people may move in your direction if it looks as though all their friends and neighbors are with you. Focus on getting signs in homes and on lawns for that personal endorsement.

- **Literature.** Budget your literature according to your ability to get it to voters. If you have three county chairpersons, with twenty volunteers each, willing to work for 10 hours each weekend, with three weekends remaining until the election, you have 600 hours of volunteer labor. If the average volunteer can deliver ten pieces of literature an hour to a home, then you should order about 18,000 pieces of literature. Never order based on what you would like to get out— only on what you can really deliver.

SAMPLE FIELD BUDGET: GET-OUT-THE-VOTE MATERIALS

This sample field budget of campaign materials may provide a feel for the allocation of funds in the final days of a campaign:

5,000 walk-pieces	$2,000
1,000 signs	$1,000
1,500 buttons	$200
500 bumper stickers	$300
3,000 door-hangers	$1,000
7,000 slate cards	$1,000
5 get-out-the-vote trainings for base communities	$1,000
Field travel expense	$500
Election Day general	$1,000

- **Campaign fashion.** Hats and T-shirts are great for motivating volunteers. They are best used to communicate an image of your campaign—excitement and energy. And by all means be sure they are made in America.

- **Bilingual materials.** In certain communities there is no substitute for reaching voters in their native language. It may be appropriate to consider communicating your message in this way. However, be careful because you can offend entire communities of voters by putting out poorly translated materials.

PLAN YOUR VOTER CONTACT

Types of voter contact. Make your choices depending on your strategic objectives. If the initiative or candidate has a low level of name identification, the campaign will educate targeted voters about the candidate and the candidate's message before voter-identification efforts begin. If the campaign has financial assets, this education can be accomplished by early media and a series of large or frequent mailings to targeted voters. If the campaign has less money, then the campaign can organize a large number of volunteers to drop literature in targeted precincts. If the campaign has a large number of volunteers and time, a series of door-to-door canvasses can help raise name identification.

The sequence of these voter contact activities is important. The campaign will not have a successful phone canvass to identify supporters if the campaign has poor name recognition. It is unwise to attack your opponent without giving people a reason to vote for you. The proper sequence of a voter contact program will vary greatly from campaign to campaign. Most campaigns concentrate the early voter contact and voter-identification programs in precincts that are low performance.

Mix your voter contact techniques: low intensity and high intensity. Low-intensity activities are not highly individualized and are not high impact. Low-intensity voter contact programs impart information about the candidate and can move voters, but they are not as persuasive as high-intensity programs. High-intensity programs are more individualized and more persuasive. High-intensity voter contact techniques often involve two-way communication. They give voters an opportunity to express their opinions about the

CREATIVE OUTREACH

The hand: In Idaho, Larry LaRocco was running for lieutenant governor. He had a card with a hand on it that read "25,000 hands/25,000 Idaho stories" that he gave to everyone. Each hand—representing a handshake—was numbered, so people felt engaged when they got #324 or #67. They would greet him by shouting, "I'm #324!" "Remember me? I'm #67." Months after the campaign, people still identified themselves by the personalized number.*

The fan: In the South, many candidates distribute "funeral fans"—named because they would be passed out at sweltering services. Originally the fans had the name of the funeral home on them; now they have candidate names and causes.

The pint: Some candidates distribute pints of liquor with their campaign information plastered on them (and possibly their volunteers plastered after drinking them)—not a wise choice but a colorful tradition. Others have adapted the nonalcoholic version: for a 2006 win-the-House event, Congresswoman Barbara Lee served up miniature champagne bottles filled with sparkling cider labeled with Speaker-to-be Nancy Pelosi's face superimposed on a Rosie the Riveter image on the label.

The song: Although each candidate will have his or her "walk on music" for large events and rallies, nothing beats a homegrown campaign song. For instance, Hank Johnson, former DeKalb County, Georgia, commissioner and now a congressman, had a song encap-

*George Miller discussion about the campaign trail highlights, November 14, 2006; Larry LaRocco, e-mail, July 23, 2007.

sulating his message entitled "Taking Care of Home." A downloadable MP3 recording of the song was on Hank Johnson's Web site.*

The video: In 1988, Anna Eshoo ran for Congress in the Silicon Valley. She put together a video, "Anna Eshoo Will Challenge the Sacred Cows." The video was the first of its kind: a pollster asked whether people had video machines, volunteers delivered 110,000 cassettes in just two weekends, and the campaign generated media buzz and voter excitement. "People thought: 'If she can think that way in how she communicates with us, imagine what she'll do when she represents us,'" remembers Eshoo. **

The personalized poster: The 2004 Bush-Cheney campaign had an interactive computer program called the Sloganator on their Web site that invited supporters to personalize their posters. People could go online and create their own personal poster for the campaign. Although the tricksters got to it, creating posters not in keeping with the campaign's messages, the two-way outreach was a great innovation.***

The nail file: In California, Rosalind Wyman ran for city council in the 1960s. She passed out nail files imprinted with her name. Years later, in races for Democratic National Committee, Wyman reprised the nail files and slogans. Although the 1996 slogan, "Let's nail down Clinton's reelection," was apt for its time, many an activist made use of the file emblazoned with "With Roz Wyman on the DNC, this election won't be a nail biter" during the recounts of 2000.

*Hank Johnson for Congress Web site: www.hankforcongress.com/multimedia/campaignsong.
**Anna Eshoo, interview, July 22, 2007.
***Daniel Kurtzman, "The Bush-Cheney Sloganator," *About.com: PoliticalHumor,* March 15, 2004, http://politicalhumor.about.com/b/a/088547.htm.

candidate and the campaign. The actual voter-identification programs—operations that organize staff or volunteers to talk to voters and ask their candidate preference and opinion on specific issues—are high-intensity programs.

Voter-identification programs allow the campaign to gather information that allows them to contact voters in a persuasive manner. For example, say your phone bank operation asked voters a number of questions about the issues they thought were most important and about who they were likely to support in the election. Many of the respondents will report themselves undecided on the election, but most will be willing to rate the issues. A high-intensity voter contact program allows you to contact those undecided voters by mail with the campaign's position on the issues they consider most important. You will concentrate your high-intensity voter contact in areas of poor party performance. These are the areas where you have to do the most persuasion (in persuadable precincts) and identify your supporters to get them out to vote.

In areas of good party performance, you will be getting everyone out to the polls on Election Day, so you will not be doing much candidate preference identification before get-out-the-vote begins. This area may be more suited for low-impact voter contact in which the campaign does not need to persuade voters. The high-intensity contact in these areas will come during the get-out-the-vote phase of the campaign.

Low-Impact Voter Contact

Literature Distribution. "Lit drops" are the most basic form of campaigning. Literature is placed in a secure area on the doors of houses in the areas you want to cover. Do not put any campaign literature in mailboxes—doing so is illegal. Volunteers do not knock on doors or talk to voters during a lit drop. You can target literature distribution by delivering literature in persuadable precincts or leaving literature only at the homes of target voters. Lit drops are volunteer- and time-intensive but do not cost a lot of money.

Leafleting. Leafleting is similar to literature distribution, but the literature is distributed at public places like shopping centers or college campuses. It is less targeted than lit drops because you have little control over who is taking your literature or where these voters live. Leafleting is a good way to hand out simple flyers for things like building a crowd for an event.

Visibility. Visibility activities are those that get the candidate's name out and raise the profile of the campaign. Usually very little message or issue information about the candidate is given out at visibility events. Examples include buttons and bumper stickers, lawn signs, billboards, and human sandwich boards.

High-Impact Voter Contact

Door-to-Door. Canvassing is one of the most traditional and effective forms of voter contact. An organized canvassing operation with well-trained volunteers yields excellent results in persuading undecided voters. On the other hand, an unorganized operation with poorly trained volunteers can be a major drain of time and resources on a campaign and may lose votes.

Phoning. Phone banks are one of the most commonly used forms of voter contact for voter identification, voter turnout, volunteer recruitment, fund-raising, and crowd building. You must decide what part phone-banking plays in your overall voter contact strategy, then determine how many phone calls must be made, how many volunteer hours it will take to complete the calls, and how they will be done (paid or volunteer). Be clear about the type of race you are in before you start your phone program. If you are simply trying to mobilize your core base of supporters to go out and vote, you probably need to only make one or two rounds of calls.

Typically, you will need to call through your lists, find un-decided voters sympathetic to your message, send them one or two mailings, and call them again to find out if they have switched to your side. Then you will still need to do your one or two rounds of calls to get people to come out and vote on Election Day.

Candidate Activity. The most effective form of voter contact is the candidate asking someone face-to-face for a vote. The candidate's time is one of the most valuable and scarcest re-sources of every campaign. All of the voter contact portion of the candidate's time should be oriented toward reaching the highest number of persuadable voters. Campaigns can also use personalized direct mail, specialized canvassing, and tar-geted media buying to personally solicit voters for their support.

House Meetings. As we saw in chapter 5, Connect with Peo-ple, every campaign begins in the community. No candidate should consider running before committing to at least one hundred house meetings. Your goal should be to recruit an average of ten volunteers from each house meeting, so that you have attracted a movement of one thousand volunteers, each of whom has heard the call to service, "kicked the tires" on the initiative or candidate, and committed to helping the service mission succeed. The team's one hundred house meeting hosts will invite neighbors and colleagues for coffee with the candidate, who visits with ten to forty people for an hour, recruiting an average of ten volunteers per house meeting. The campaign should provide the host with a house meeting kit that includes invitations to a list of voters in the area. A sample house meeting kit may include the following: invitations, buttons, literature, volunteer cards, contribution envelopes, and thank-you letters.

Town meetings. Similar to a house meeting but held in a larger, more public place with more people, town meetings have a more formal presentation format. Town meetings are therefore less personal and more publicly oriented.

Door-to-door. Door-to-door can be made more efficient by having a number of people advance the candidate by dropping literature before she gets to the neighborhood. It also helps to have a few people walk down the street with the candidate to help the candidate move along and identify people who are home and want to meet the candidate. The campaign should track the voters the candidate meets and generate follow-up letters. The campaign should generate press about taking the campaign to the people.

Town or Main Street tours. If you are working with a candidate, set up candidate walks down the street meeting people and shaking hands accompanied by a local community leader or small-business owner.

Preset events (you are invited). It is often worthwhile to attend events (dinners, fairs, meetings, and so forth) where the lead organizer, campaign team, or candidate has been asked

COMPONENTS OF A SUCCESSFUL HOUSE MEETING STRATEGY

Your strategy includes these components: house meeting coordinators, hosts, message, goals, script, materials, scheduling, feedback, and follow-up.

Coordinators. Your team's house meeting coordinators will recruit hosts, put together house meeting packets, map out where meetings are held, keep track of how many volunteers are recruited, report guests' feedback, and handle campaign follow-up. A handful of well-trained volunteers can perform this function as a team, with responsibility divided along geographic or political lines across the community.

Hosts. Start with your networks: your family, friends, work colleagues, and nonprofit allies. Looking at your community inventory, enlist leaders from organizations that are active in civic and political life. If you don't know the leaders well, consider your allies to recruit people who have a history of hosting house meetings for causes and candidates who share your public service mission. Look broadly: a house meeting doesn't even need to be in a house. Some people don't feel comfortable having people they don't know come into their home but are happy to host a meeting at a community center, a local coffee house, or a campus deli. The key is to have a comfortable meeting place where people can come together in their own neighborhood or precinct for an hour and learn about the campaign.

Message. This is your best opportunity to meet people, present your campaign plan, and recruit volunteers. People will be looking for your call to service: the vision, ideas, and values that shape an individual candidacy or a ballot initiative.

Goals. Set goals based on your targeting. In a campaign that needs one thousand volunteers, you will need to recruit an average of ten people from one hundred house meetings. Hosts who know you well or who are involved with large organizations will be asked to target a higher level of recruitment.

Script. Prepare a template for your house meeting script. First, the host welcomes participants. Second, participants introduce themselves and tell why they are there. Third, the campaign leader or candidate talks about the message and the candidate and asks people to get involved in the campaign. This program may involve a multimedia presentation such as a DVD of campaign ads or testimonials. Fourth, the host leads a discussion where the candidate takes questions. Fifth, every house meeting should end with thanks and requests for support.

Materials. Each host needs a host packet containing campaign information (DVD, issue summary or candidate biography, sample invitations, literature, and noteworthy news articles) and volunteer cards.

Scheduling. Your scheduler, coordinators, and hosts should work together to create a master schedule for house meetings. Many campaigns have this information online so that people who enter their zip code can identify upcoming meetings in their area. You may also plan one night of many house meetings with a conference call from an all-star to boost the campaign.

Feedback. After each meeting, the host should meet with her coordinator to report on the meeting and to give feedback that can be used to determine whether changes are needed. Consider these factors: turnout, program, and systems. Ask what can be done to ensure that more people get there. Ask if people understand the message and campaign plan. Ask whether new recruits feel welcome.

Follow-up. The candidate or initiative campaign leader should send a thank-you note to the host and should contact each new donor, volunteer, or potential host. Add their names to your e-mail list and volunteer database. Be sure to follow up on any questions (such as the candidate's stance on a particular issue or the policy triggers that affect a ballot initiative) or requests (such as house signs or additional literature).

to speak. There is a built-in crowd, so your challenge is to generate press coverage of your message and to get volunteer recruitment from the event.

Created events (you invite voters). Speaking to a group of students or teachers about drugs or education, meeting with nurses at a hospital and discussing health care, going to a toxic waste site to talk about groundwater—all have a better chance of getting the campaign earned media, especially TV. Make sure you have sign-up sheets and volunteers with clipboards to gather names of attendees to contact later for support.

Rallies. Rallies are campaign gatherings where the candidate speaks or surrogates speak on behalf of the candidate, especially in the closing days of the campaign. It is more likely that rallies will occur in larger races. Rallies take a great deal of time and money to set up, so maximize your resources by pairing rallies with trainings or field events. Press coverage of the rally is critical, but be sure to bring out the people, because a small crowd can get you a bad story.

Feedback. Follow-up is the chariot of success. Voters have questions, and volunteers offer time; follow-up is what will drive them toward your campaign. Here is where an *open feedback loop* is essential: voters will be giving information to your volunteers who in turn will convey it to your campaign. There must be a venue for the candidate to hear what voters think of the candidacy and the message, and to provide answers and feedback. Voters' concerns will range from microissues, such as a particular bill, which a follow-up phone call can answer, to macroissues, such as a character attack slung by the opposition, which warrants a much more publicly broadcast response. Either way, voters will expect you to respond to them. Be sure to use your kitchen cabinet, house meeting hosts, finance council, volunteer corps, and election protection team to receive input as to what questions are out there and what responses are (or are not) resonating.

PLAN YOUR GET-OUT-THE-VOTE STRATEGY

Early voting. In many communities, voter registrars allow people to vote up to thirty days before Election Day. This means that canvassing must include an early voting strategy. If you have a good voter file, you can identify people, input their addresses into the system, and send them an e-mail at the start of early voting. Shortly before the election, cross-check the voter file against the list of voters who have already voted. If your targeted supporters are not recorded as voting, send them another e-mail the weekend before the election.

Snowbirds and other seasonal residents. In Florida, many voters are "snowbirds"—people who reside in the southland during the winter months to escape the cold weather. Congressman Ron Klein targeted them through a field organization and database. Klein's field director developed a program to reach snowbirds at their homes outside Florida. Klein's campaign also tried to identify residents of gated communities that are off-limits to candidates and canvassers in order to recruit volunteers within the walls. Klein canvassers contacted sixty thousand identified Klein voters in the final three days; on the Friday before the election alone, the campaign reached seven thousand people by phone or in person.[12]

Vote-by-mail/absentee ballot. Voters who cast their votes through the mail have a major impact on elections in many states. States first embraced vote-by-mail initiatives as a way to boost declining voter turnout. Other states expanded the use of absentee ballots from the homebound, temporarily out of town, or overseas military personnel to all citizens. Check the rules of your state and plan accordingly.

A good vote-by-mail/absentee-ballot program requires your campaign to identify your supporters, target those with a weak voting history and those who have voted by mail in the past, and walk those voters through the process of casting their ballots by mail. This process generally means mailing and calling voters several times. Before launching a vote-by-mail program, you must have a reliable method to track the voters you have targeted.

Start with the voter file you purchased to prepare your community inventory. Then update your file with information from your community inventory, networks, commercially available data, and canvassing contacts. Get an updated list from the voter registrar to include people who have registered to vote since you began this process.

If your polling or other research indicates that your initiative or candidate has strong support among the most infrequent voters, you may choose to immediately target this group for your vote-by-mail program. Otherwise, you will probably start with canvassing and phone calls to identify supporters who do not frequently vote.

The key is to conduct a sustained conversation between the campaign and your target voters. This may mean mailing to the group several times and then following up with phone calls to make sure their ballots have actually been mailed. A final phone call should remind those who have not already returned their ballots to vote in person on Election Day. As with every other part of the campaign, your goal should be to walk the voters through the entire vote-by-mail process, making things as easy for them as possible.

Study the different voting patterns among the absentee voters. Divide absentee voters into two categories and track them separately: (1) people who always get absentee ballots and always vote; (2) people who always get absentee ballots but do not always vote. Obviously, the second group needs a bigger push to send in their ballots. When ballots are mailed out to absentee voters (usually four weeks before the election), canvass to encourage people to send in their ballots. Later, in the final days before the election, canvass the people who have not voted and encourage them to mail or drop off their ballots at their polling places.

Your city or county might allow you to mail large numbers of vote-by-mail applications to voters. If you have the resources, you should definitely take advantage of this opportunity. An additional benefit of a well-run vote-by-mail program can be to inoculate your campaign against last-minute attacks.

Your goal should be to start Election Day with as many votes already cast as possible. Start with a good list of registered voters who have voted absentee in the past. Send at least one and preferably more mail pieces to your absentee targets. Send potential absentee voters whatever paperwork or form they need to file in order to receive an absentee ballot in the mail. Make sure postage is paid for them to mail the application. (Check the exact requirements for your community as to what these forms need to look like, whether they need to be state forms or can be a duplicate, and so forth) Call these voters to make sure they have completed their application and, later, to make sure they have mailed in their actual ballot.

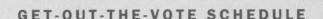

GET-OUT-THE-VOTE SCHEDULE

One month prior to Election Day

- Canvassers identify enough voters to meet their vote goals.
- Based on canvass results, choose target areas for the Election Day operation (put workers in strong areas where they can get the most supporters to the polls).
- Sign up two-thirds of the Election Day volunteers needed for get-out-the-vote plan.
- Choose a location for Election Day training and/or final rally.
- Set content of Election Day materials for captains, pollwatchers, and workers.
- Make a complete list of all polling places.
- Place printing order for Election Day sample ballots and door-hangers.
- Set location of victory party.

Three weeks before Election Day

- Organize Election Day volunteers by precinct.
- Produce copies of Election Day training packet.
- Canvassers speak to undecided voters and people voting with absentee ballots.
- Identify sites where phone calls can be made during Election Day.

Two weeks before Election Day

- Have Election Day materials in the campaign office sorted by precinct.
- Voter lists are prepared for precinct captains and pollwatchers.
- Purchase polling place materials: supplies, tape, pens, and so forth.

Ten days prior to Election Day

- Train Election Day workers and volunteers.
- Precinct captains and pollwatchers get an Election Day training kit to read.
- Captains receive a list of supporters as well as signs, staplers, tape, and pens. They also get a list of volunteers assigned to them.
- Election Day workers get their precinct assignments.

Two days prior to Election Day

- Captains and volunteers prepare for get-out-the-vote on Election Day.
- Captains call the volunteers assigned to them to confirm and check who needs a ride.

Election Day

- Pollwatchers arrive at 5:30 a.m. and supervise the preparations to open the polls.
- Volunteers place door-hangers at homes of voters, avoiding homes with dogs if possible—no need to wake the neighbors!

6 a.m.—polls open

- Pollwatchers and passers are in place.
- Pollwatchers begin crossing off names, and passers begin handing out sample ballots.
- Precinct captains phone in to headquarters and give a status report.
- Captains then buy coffee and doughnuts for their workers.

9 a.m.—calls begin

- Phone calls to supporters start from various locations and continue throughout the day.

(continued)

GET-OUT-THE-VOTE SCHEDULE

(continued)

10 a.m.—first run

• Pollwatcher gives precinct captain the names of all identified voters who have not voted.

• Precinct captain gives cards to drivers, who visit supporters' homes and give election reminders.

• Precinct captain calls the office to ensure everything is going smoothly and then buys breakfast for the volunteers.

• Field director may give orders to move volunteers according to pollwatcher results.

2 p.m.

• Pollwatcher gives precinct captain the names of all identified voters who have not voted.

• Precinct captain gives cards to drivers, who visit supporters' homes and give election reminders.

• Precinct captain calls the office.

• Field director may give orders to move volunteers according to pollwatcher results.

CONVENE A CAMPAIGN TEAM BOOT CAMP
TO LOCK IN OR ADJUST YOUR TACTICS

Public service campaigns are marathons. They take months to build before the public tunes in. If a marathon is 26.2 miles, the public is tuning in at mile 24; just when you are getting tired,

5 p.m.

- Pollwatcher gives precinct captain the names of all identified voters who have not voted.
- Precinct captain gives cards to drivers, who visit supporters' homes and give election reminders.
- Precinct captain calls the office.
- Field director may move volunteers to precincts with lower turnout according to pollwatcher results.

6 p.m.

- Pollwatcher gives precinct captain the names of all identified voters who have not voted.
- Precinct captain gives cards to drivers, who drive any remaining voters to the polls.

8 p.m.

- Pollwatcher and precinct captain remain until every voter in line has an opportunity to vote.
- Volunteers clean up signs and campaign literature around the polls.

9 p.m.—Victory Party

- Pollwatcher and precinct captain observe the ballot counting and let election protection team know of any difficulties.

Source: AFSCME and New House PAC, "AFSCME/New House PAC: 2006 Congressional Candidates Boot Camp Manual."

people are waking up to your race. Be sure you get a fresh look at what they will see. Set aside some time approximately seventy-five days before Election Day to convene a campaign boot camp to lock in a winner or adjust while you can.

With your team, perform the exercises from each of the

chapters to assess and update. Take an honest measure of your campaign. Hope is not a strategy. You cannot plan to win because you hope to raise money or connect with people at this late date; rather, you have to base your final planning on what you actually have accomplished and build from there. Review the seven steps of the Boot Camp to lock in or adjust your tactics:

1. *Identify your call to service:* Retake the public service fitness test and see if your campaign reflects your campaign's public service mission. Are you fulfilling the promises and commitments you made? Did the campaign leadership commit the necessary time, energy, resources, and reputation? If not, what would you change? How is family life? Is everyone still on board? Does the campaign reflect the vision, ideas, and values that inspire the call to service?

2. *Know your community:* Has the campaign visited every possible neighborhood? Do you have the demographic breakdown, financial information, and voter data? Do you have political support in each of the neighborhoods of your community? Does your campaign reflect the concerns and aspirations of the people? Have you planned get-out-the-vote events at those traditional community events you inventoried?

3. *Build your leadership teams:* Do you have the people in place to succeed? Did the candidate or lead organizer fully commit herself and hire people who work well together? How has the kitchen cabinet handled surprises and setbacks? Are the house meeting hosts having events and building the volunteer corps? Did the finance council raise the funds needed to implement the campaign plan? Do you have a vibrant volunteer corps? Is the election

protection team in place, with an inventory of eligible voters, voting systems, and resources needed to count every vote as cast?

4. *Define your message:* Is your message getting out there? How have allies and attacks affected people's perceptions of the campaign? Is there anything you need to change here?

5. *Connect with people:* Have you reached the people where they live? Are there any debate positives to broadcast or gaffes to overcome? What is your online presence? Who have been your best allies and validators, and are they available in the next seventy-five days to help?

6. *Raise the money:* Did people come through? Did the money calls get made? Why or why not? Are there people you can still pull in before the filing deadline to fund the last push? Should you add more fund-raising at house meetings or call time to get the funds needed to meet the budget? If not, your team needs to adjust the plans according to what is real, not what you hope.

7. *Mobilize to win:* Have you recruited a volunteer corps and mobilized supporters to your cause? Where can you conduct more house meetings? What networks might you tap for additional support?

GET-OUT-THE-VOTE RALLIES: BRING IN THE ALL-STARS

The final days of a campaign sum up what the election is all about. If you are running for office or volunteering on a campaign, now is the time to bring your people together and persuade voters to go to the polls. To get last-minute media attention and rally the troops, bring in the all-stars.

On the campaign trail in 2006, President George W. Bush and First Lady Laura Bush stumped for Republicans, while former President Bill Clinton and former Vice President Al Gore stumped for Democrats. Their appearances sum up the message of the campaigns:

First Lady Laura Bush spent the last days before the election at congressional campaign rallies in Kentucky and Ohio, while President Bush traveled to Georgia and Texas. On the Saturday before the election, President Bush held a telephone conference call with about three thousand Republican local officials to fire them up for a final get-out-the-vote push, and on Monday, Bush invited Fox News talk show host Sean Hannity for a ride on Air Force One.

President Bush also called in to the Rush Limbaugh radio show with his take on the election: "I believe if our candidates continue to talk about the strong economy, based upon low taxes, and an administration and a Congress that was willing to give professionals the tools necessary to protect [citizens from terrorism] we'll win this election." Bush responded to questions about Iraq war critics this way: "My answer to them is listen to Osama bin Laden who says, 'Our objective is to defeat America,' which will embolden the terrorists, which will then enable [al-Qaeda] to have safe haven, just like they had in Afghanistan. And we're not going to let them do it."[13]

Meanwhile, from the front porch of civil rights icon and Congressman John Lewis's Georgia home, President Clinton said: "The Republican campaign slogan seems to be: 'you gotta vote for us—they'll tax you into the poorhouse and have a terrorist on every street corner as you walk there.' Now this election is about major challenges. This imposes a tremendous burden on us. We cannot just talk to our base— we need to talk to Republican and Independent voters too.

This election is about reclaiming America's fundamental purpose: the common good."[14]

A week later, during a Pennsylvania bus tour, came a passionate plea from former Vice Presient Al Gore at the Cabrini College gymnasium: "People are ahead of their politicians in recognizing the climate crisis and pursuing solutions. . . . This election, we will breathe new life into American democracy. We will limit the influence of greedy special interests. We will send men and women to honor the oath of office to defend the Constitution. We will send men and women to represent 'we the people.'"[15]

For candidates, the all-stars bring a final boost to campaign efforts. For volunteers, this is a reward for hard work and a motivator for the last push to the polls. For voters, it is an opportunity to see the individual campaign in a larger perspective. Note what the all-stars said and where they said it: the first lady at congressional rallies; the president on conservative radio; former President Clinton at the home of a civil rights icon; former Vice President Gore on a bus tour through a swing state.

THE HOME STRETCH: DEMONSTRATE STAMINA AND LEADERSHIP

It is also the time to stay focused: at the end of a marathon, people are tired and are more likely to make mistakes or lose focus. A disciplined campaign runs like they are behind even when polls say they are ahead; they stay focused and use rapid response to counter late hits. As a candidate, campaign worker, or issue advocate, you will have to demonstrate stamina and leadership in the final pressure-filled days.

Even if things appear to be going your way, you must take

nothing for granted. In late October 2006, Congressman Heath Shuler, a former NFL quarterback running for office in Waynesville, North Carolina, was recruiting volunteers and voters despite enjoying a big lead. His volunteer coordinator told me, "The polls say we are ten points up but we are running like we're ten points down."

HALT. Take heed to stay focused in the final days. Candidates and volunteers often go without sleep or get nervous, and that's when a gaffe can derail the best of campaigns. In the recovery movement, they say that people are most likely to relapse when they are hungry, angry, lonely, or tired.

In that spirit, think "HALT"—and literally halt. If you are hungry, eat something. If you are angry, shrug off political attacks rather than taking them personally. If you are lonely (politically speaking), reach out to a broader audience and connect with people who are there to help the campaign come together. If you are tired, get some sleep. In the last few days, candidates may be asked trick questions that will end up blanketing the airwaves, so be especially careful that you, as a candidate, volunteer, or issue advocate, have the presence of mind to HALT and display grace under pressure.

Remember to throw a punch and take a punch. In the final weekend of any political campaign, this may be the difference between winning and losing.

On the Friday morning before the 2000 election, at a time when candidates Al Gore and George W. Bush were running even in the polls, news broke about Bush's 1976 drunk-driving criminal conviction in Maine. The Bush team had a three-pronged rapid response: put Bush in front of the cameras, push back on unsavory elements of the story, and blame the leak on Gore supporters. First, Bush said: "Obviously there's a report out tonight that twenty-four years ago, I was apprehended in Kennebunkport, Maine, for a DWI. That's an accurate story. I'm not proud of that." Second, when a dispute arose as to whether or not Bush had lied to Texas reporter Wayne Slater by not revealing the DWI conviction when Slater asked if Bush had ever been arrested, Bush adviser Karen Hughes, who had been present at the interview, maintained that she had "stopped the conversation" before the issue could arise. Third, Bush supporters hit Gore, blaming him for the leak.[16]

Not only did the Gore campaign not know of Bush's conviction (so they obviously were in no position to leak it), they found the leak to be a distraction to their candidate. The Gore campaign found out who the leaker was and told the press. "The Bush people were very good about saying this is a dirty trick (even when, as in the earlier case of the leaked Bush practice debate tapes, it was not a Gore campaign leak)," remembers Donnie Fowler who served as Gore's 2000 field director. "While Gore advisers spent precious time trying to track down the leaker, " Fowler recalls, "Bush advisers went on the attack, blaming Gore anyway, and further putting the Gore campaign back on its heels with only four days to go."[17]

The lesson here: the campaign that can take a punch, absorb the hit, and throw a punch in response can turn the tables on the opposition.

This lesson was applied in the closing days of the 2006 campaign. The punches about Iraq kept on coming as did the rapid response: "To pull out, to withdraw from this war is losing. The Democrats appear to be content with losing," said Senator Elizabeth Dole of North Carolina, who led the Senate GOP's campaign efforts. Infuriated, Rahm Emanuel, Democratic Congressional Campaign Committee chairman, responded: "We want to win and we want a new direction for Iraq."[18]

ELECTION DAY

When supportive voters wake up on Election Day, there is a message hanging on their doorknobs to remind them to go to the polls. As they arrive at the polling place, volunteers hand out sample ballots. The pollwatcher has made sure that everything inside is set up properly and begins keeping track of everyone who votes. When the voter arrives, a pollwatcher marks that person off a list of registered voters. At 10 a.m., the pollwatcher gives the precinct captain the index cards for supporters who have not voted. Drivers then visit the homes of those voters and leave a second reminder about the election. This process is repeated at 2 p.m., 5 p.m., and a final time at 6 p.m. Based on the information provided by pollwatchers, campaign staff and volunteers may be moved throughout the day to target areas with low turnout.

Meanwhile, one person for each area is making calls to all supporters, reminding them to get out and vote. These calls start at 9 a.m. and continue throughout the day. When the polls close, the pollwatcher and precinct captain supervise the ballot counting, phone the results in to the campaign office, and then head over to the victory party.

To run a good Election Day operation, you need an election protection team consisting of a field director, precinct captains, pollwatchers, passers, drivers, phoners, and office staff in place. These are their assignments.

Your Election Protection Team

These lawyers and legal observers should be available and on call for precinct work. They can take information by cell phone and camcorder recordings of incidents and work with election incident clearinghouses. As to the mechanics of your election protection team, Donna Brazile counsels: "The

election protection team's primary responsibility is to anticipate and address uninformed poll workers, new voting systems, purges of voter registration lists, voter suppression,
misinformation, and intimidation tactics. The team needs to
be in place early to ensure the elections are being adminis-
trated in a fair and transparent manner. The more issues
that can be addressed in advance, the more access voters will
have to the process. An election protection team is one way
of making sure that everyone who can vote has their vote
counted."[19]

Your election protection team is responsible for promoting civic participation and a stronger democracy through ensuring every citizen's right to vote. You will want to be sure
that your team is connected with the national parties' voting
inforation centers. "The more people who vote, the better it
is for our country," declares Democratic National Committee
Chairman Howard Dean on the party's Web site. "That is
why we have the most comprehensive national election protection program ever, ensuring people can vote with confidence in all 50 states."[20]

Your team should place attorneys specializing in election
law on hand to answer any questions coming in from the
pollwatchers or precinct captains. In the case of disputes, it
helps to have an attorney available to send to a precinct if
there is a problem.

Field director. Your campaign must make adjustments
throughout the day in response to information coming in
from the field. This may mean shifting volunteers to areas
when large numbers of your supporters are not showing up
to vote. Ultimately, these types of decisions should be made
by one person, typically the field director, rather than being
left to the discretion of each individual precinct captain.

Precinct captains. Each precinct captain must be your field general who makes sure that operations run smoothly, that all resources are being used correctly, and that the office is notified immediately of any potential problems. Specific responsibilities of the precinct captain include making sure that all volunteers get to the polling place on time, that the polls open and close on time, that all volunteers get a breakfast snack and lunch, and that all identified voters get to the polls to vote. It is absolutely critical that your precinct captains be reliable. You must test them at various intervals throughout the campaign to find out which ones will perform and which will not. You cannot simply make assumptions based on their history of support. Precinct captains should also be asked to call their numbers in to the office when the polls open, at 10 a.m., 2 p.m., 5 p.m., and after the polls close.

Pollwatchers. This is the most important job inside the polling place on Election Day. Your election protection team has met, identified the problem areas, set up a phone number for troubleshooters, and is poised for action. The pollwatcher must be capable of keeping track of everyone who votes. You must have an accurate list of all supporters who have not voted so you can get these people to the polls. This person is also responsible for making sure all voting is done in a fair manner.

Pollwatchers must be familiar with election law and somewhat aggressive to be able to challenge any suspicious activities. They must start the day by making sure that the ballot box is empty before voters begin arriving and finish the day by helping the precinct captain supervise the ballot counting. Because this is a tedious, all-day job, it is best to have a morning and an afternoon pollwatcher for each precinct. Pollwatching is also a technical job, so these people will need training from your election protection team.

Passers. There should be a minimum of two people assigned to each polling place who are responsible for visibility. These people start their day by making sure your signs are in place around the polling place one hour before the polls open. They finish their day by making sure that all campaign signs have been removed. During voting hours, they should be stationed outside at or near the polling place to pass out your literature and sample ballots. Note: consult your state election law for any restrictions on passing out literature at or near the polling place.

Drivers. At least one (and preferably two) people should be assigned as drivers to each precinct or area. These people may also serve as passers, but their primary function is to pick up supportive people who need a ride to vote. During the day, the precinct captain should give them a list of names of nonvoting supporters at 10 a.m., 2 p.m., and 5 p.m. The list will be provided by the pollwatcher. The drivers will then visit each house on the list, remind the people to vote, and offer them a ride to the polling place.

Phoners. You should have at least one person making phone calls from a house or office in each precinct throughout the day. This person should be calling all supporters and reminding them to vote. The calls can start as early as 8 a.m. and should continue throughout the day.

Office staff. Everyone should be in the field with only a skeleton staff at the headquarters to make sure that things are flowing smoothly and to patch holes where there are problems.

Protect the Vote

First, know your voters. Your goal is to be sure that all your voters come out to the polls, vote for your cause or candidate, and have their votes be counted as cast. So you need to know who is registered, who is eligible, what voter identification if any they need to bring to the polls, and whether they are permanent absentee voters (meaning they will be dropping off their ballot at the polls). By identifying supporters and gaining up-to-date voter registration lists, you will have a sense of who is eligible to vote in that precinct. If same-day registration is allowed, you will need to know the eligibility requirements.

Second, know your voting rights. The three most basic voting protections to remind voters are these: first, you have a right to view a sample ballot at the polling place before voting; second, if you are in line before the published closing time, you are entitled to cast a ballot; and third, if you have problems, you are still entitled to cast a provisional ballot.

Third, know your ballot. With several races on the ballot at once, you will want voters to find your candidate or ballot initiative easily. If your candidate is running against a dozen people for city council and voters can pick up to three choices, let them know that in advance. If your community has ranked choice or instant runoff voting, be sure your supporters and pollwatchers have explained the process to your voters. Finally, if you have paper ballots, be sure that people know to vote on the front and back sides of the ballot. It would be a shame to draw people out to the polls for a "down-ballot race" (a candidate or initiative literally situated down the ballot from the top-tier races for higher office), only to have them miss your race!

Fourth, know your voting systems. Your election protection team will have a list of the types of voting machines (paper ballots, punch cards, touch screens, optical scanners, and so forth) used at each precinct. That way, your pollwatchers know the types of equipment being used for casting and counting ballots and the challenges unique to particular systems. Your team will want to know what machinery is being used; any research regarding possible tampering and computer malfunctions, particularly with the touch screens; and whether there are sufficient protections for disabled voters so that, pursuant to federal law, they are enabled to vote independently. Rather than training everyone about every kind of voting system, be efficient and target your trainings. In a congressional district with five counties, you might have five different kinds of voting systems, so be sure your inventory is accurate and that you conduct five distinct trainings—one per county.

Fifth, know your legal options. A smooth election protection operation allows pollwatchers and hotlines to solve election problems before provisional ballots are cast. When your pollwatchers identify problems, they should contact a member of your election protection team who can work on the problem—and even call a judge if necessary. Better to work out the challenge beforehand if possible, rather than adding a vote to the pile of provisional votes that may or may not ever be counted.

Sixth, document everything. In case of a recount or challenge, sworn affidavits and cell phone videos of the challenges make the evidence more tangible. In the end, your election records should demonstrate that your team took exquisite care to ensure that the laws were followed and that the votes were counted as cast.

The goal is to wake up after Election Day with no regrets. You have performed according to the highest ideals of your call to service, you have excelled at the management, message, money, and mobilization (avoiding lessons learned and creating a few new examples of best practices of your own), and done your best to make sure that everyone has voted and that all the votes were counted as cast.

GET REAL: BOOT CAMP CHECKLIST

As you head into the last seventy-five days of the campaign marathon, convene a campaign boot camp to lock in a winner or readjust as needed. Gather your team together and consider the following:

1. *Identify your call to service:*

- Retake the public service test: does your campaign reflect your service mission?
- Are you fulfilling the promises and commitments you made?
- Did you commit the necessary time, energy, resources, and reputation?
- If not, what would you change?
- How is family life? Is everyone still on board?
- Does the campaign reflect the vision, ideas, and values that inspire the call to service?

2. *Know your community:*

- Has the campaign visited every possible neighborhood?
- Do you have the demographic breakdown, financial information, and voter data?
- Have you identified your winning number and can you reach that goal?

3. Build your leadership teams:

- Do you have the people in place to succeed?
- Did the candidate or lead organizer fully commit herself and hire people who work well together?
- How has the kitchen cabinet handled surprises and setbacks?
- Are the house meeting hosts having events and building the volunteer corps?
- Do you have a vibrant volunteer corps?
- Did the finance council raise the funds needed to implement the campaign plan?
- Is the election protection team in place?

4. Define your message:

- Is your message getting out there?
- How have allies and attacks affected people's perceptions of the campaign?
- Anything you need to change here?

5. Connect with people:

- Have you reached the people where they live?
- Any debate positives to broadcast or gaffes to overcome?
- What is your online presence?
- Who have been your best allies and validators? Are they available in the next seventy-five days to help?

6. Raise the money:

- Did people come through?
- Did the money calls get made? Why or why not?

- Are there people you can still pull in before the filing deadline to fund the last push?
- Should you add more fund-raising at house meetings or call time to get the funds needed to meet the budget?
- What is your adjusted plan — according to what is real, not what you hoped to raise?

7. Mobilize to win:

- Have you recruited a volunteer corps and mobilized supporters to your cause?
- Where can you conduct more house meetings?
- What networks might you tap for additional support?
- Has your election protection team prepared your volunteers to get out the vote and be sure votes are counted as cast?

Afterword

YOU'VE WON! NOW WHAT?

You have exercised your right to vote and your commitment to service; now the marathon is over, the teamwork has paid off, and the voters have spoken. You've won—now what? Four keys to success: assume the position, stay close to your people, keep your word, and pay it forward.

Assume the position. Having heeded the call to service and succeeded on the path to service, you now have a responsibility to service that permeates your actions. It may mean conducting yourself differently than you did as a challenger or candidate. Though a faction elected you, you now represent everyone in your community. If you are a representative at any level of government, remember Speaker Pelosi's adage, and *be* a representative: vote with your constituents' interests and perform casework for everyone.

Stay close to your people. Give constant updates, interviews, and progress reports to your people. Start with a listening tour the minute you succeed. If your ballot initiative passes, keep the public, and your supporters in particular, updated when the new law goes into effect or when its benchmarks are reached. When, for example, the lower fees go into effect, the veterans get their job training assistance, the first responders get their expanded health benefits, or the tax rebates are issued, people should be able to see the impact of your work.

Keep your word. From the moment you take the oath of office, keep your word. If you promised to forego certain perks, act accordingly. If you promised to show up at all the meetings, be present and be prepared. If you promised to post your schedule on your Web site, do so. If you promised to hold public meetings, do so. Nothing un-elects people faster than breaking their word. You came into office to do something, not to be something: now is your opportunity to do so. Walk that talk.

Pay it forward. You worked hard to get here, so relish the opportunity you have to fulfill your service. In return, you have the satisfaction of being able to do something for people, to strengthen your networks, and to encourage the next generation of leaders. Somewhere in your community, a future leader is already walking in your footsteps. Be sure to bring them along when you start your next service mission.

Acknowledgments

Thanks to all the people I have met on the campaign trail since those early days in the stroller. Special thanks to the friends and mentors I met growing up in politics, who taught me how to fight, how to win, how to regroup, and how to persevere. You shaped the insights that went into the making of this book, and the campaign advice that I hope will inform a new generation of leaders.

Special thanks to those who took time from your own service to our country to lend the benefit of your thinking by contributing interviews and insights for the book. As progressives, conservatives, and muckrakers, you do not share a common philosophy, but you do share a similar belief in the power of individuals to shape history and the need for more people to become fully engaged in our democracy. I particularly appreciate the wisdom of my grassroots and netroots allies who are thriving in this new era of asymmetrical politics, bringing old school politics and new media together.

Thanks to the excellent candidates who run for office, putting yourselves out there for what you believe and trying to make a difference for the rest of us. The campaign lessons here are built on the work of the team at AFSCME who help prepare people to fight for people who work for a living: they include Gerald McEntee, Lee Saunders, Larry Scanlon, Linda Canan Stephens, Ricky Feller, and Seth Johnson. Thanks to them and to the campaign mavens at the New House PAC, including Jim Gonzalez, John Thiella, and Claude Everhardt, for elevating candidate trainings to an art form. This book would not have been possible without my networks, especially the "HUD women" from Washington, D.C.; my former Capitol Hill colleagues; my DNC colleagues and cofounders of the DNC Veterans and Military Families outreach effort; my California grassroots allies; and my baseball pals. Special thanks to the Fighting Dems and the fiercely independent vets at IAVA led by Paul Rieckhoff.

Many thanks to the publishing team at PoliPoint Press, particularly Peter Richardson, Scott Jordan, and Jonathan Harris, for their patience, smarts, and creativity. Deep appreciation to Mike Mollett, Dave Peattie, and the BookMatters team, as well as to photographer Drew Altizer. Special thanks to Lizbeth Hasse, Markos Kounalakis, and Brad Martin for their advice and counsel.

As always, lots of love to my family, for all you are and all you do.

Notes

CHAPTER 1

1. George F. Will, column, *Washington Post*, September 11, 2002; e-mail, May 17, 2007.

2. National Commission on Terrorist Attack upon the United State, *The 9/11 Commission Report*, http://www.9-11commission.gov, p. 20.

3. Nancy Pelosi, interview, July 14, 207.

4. Lezlee Westine, interview, June 12, 2007.

5. Ibid.

6. Dotty LeMieux, e-mail, May 19, 2007; "The Ties that Bind: Successful Coalition Building for Referendum or Initiative Campaigns," *Campaigns & Elections*, August 2005.

7. Mary Hughes, interview, April 10, 2007.

8. Jack Valenti, remarks (National Italian American Foundation, Washington, D.C., June 3, 2004).

9. Tim Roemer, "Winning Lessons in Red States for Blue Candidates," *Trail Mix*, May 23, 2006.

10. Jan Brown, e-mail, July 2007; remarks to Take Back Red California event, San Francisco, September 24, 2006.

11. Jennifer L. Lawless, and Richard L. Fox, "Why Don't Women Run for Office?" Brown University Policy Report, January 2004.

12. Ellen Malcolm, interview, June 29, 2007.

CHAPTER 2

1. Mary Hughes, interview, April 10, 2007.
2. Gerald W. McEntee, interview, April 25, 2007.
3. Will Easton, e-mail, May 31, 2007.
4. Phillip Carter, e-mail, May 24, 2007.
5. The Club for Growth Web site: clubforgrowth.org.
6. Greenberg & Associates poll, e-mailed, April 11, 2007.
7. Celinda Lake, interview, April 22, 2007.
8. Bruce Braley for Congress Web site: www.brucebraley.com.
9. Mike Thompson, conference call, September 15, 2005.
10. Markos Moulitsas, e-mail, June 25 2007.
11. Ibid.
12. Tim Tagaris, e-mail, June 2, 2007; "My ATM Pin Number — Or Fundraising On-line," MyDD blog, December 23, 2004, http://www.mydd.com/ story/2004/12/23/114450/18
13. Peter Wallsten and Tom Hamburger, "Two Parties Far Apart in Turnout Tactics Too," *Los Angeles Times*, November 6, 2006.
14. Donnie Fowler, interview, May 16, 2007.
15. Ibid.
16. Alex Clemens, interview, April 11, 2007.

CHAPTER 3

1. Larry Margasak, "Foley Resigns from Congress over E-mails," *Associated Press*, September 30, 2006.
2. Jim Gonzalez, e-mail, May 30, 2007.
3. Excerpted from Fred Ross, foreword to *Cesar Chavez: Autobiography of La Causa*, by Jacques E. Levy (Minneapolis: University of Minnesota Press, 2007), reprinted by permission of the University of Minnesota Press.
4. Larry Scanlon, speech (May 25, 2007).
5. Jamal Simmons, interview, May 16, 2007.
6. Dotty LeMieux, e-mail, May 21, 2007; "Ten Common Mistakes Novice Candidates Make: Myths and Facts to Help the First Time Candidate Get Off to a Sound Start," *Campaigns & Elections*, June 2003.

7. Lezlee Westine, interview, June 12, 2007.

8. Donna Brazile, e-mail, June 4, 2007.

CHAPTER 4

1. Joe Sestak, speech (Cabrini College, Radnor Township, PA, November 3, 2006).

2. Kirsten Gillibrand for Congress Web site: www.kirsten gillibrand.com; speech (San Francisco, May 31, 2007).

3. Jerry McNerney for Congress Web site: www.jerrymcnerney .com.

4. Jamal Simmons, interview, May 16, 2007.

5. Mary Hughes, interview, April 10, 2007.

6. Dotty LeMieux, e-mail, May 18, 2007.

7. Carl Pope, interview, March 27, 2007.

8. Ibid.

9. Frank Luntz, Web site: www.luntz.com/where_overview .html.

10. George Lakoff, interview, June 12, 2007.

11. Fred Ross Sr., "Axioms for Organizers," published by Service Employees International Union, 2003.

12. Kerry Kennedy, interview, April 4, 2007.

13. Chris Murphy for Congress Web site: www.murphyfor congress.org.

14. Bruce Braley for Congress Web site: www.brucebraley .com.

15. Willie L. Brown Jr., interview, March 27, 2007.

16. Ibid.

17. John F. Tierney, e-mail, June 7, 2007.

18. Michael Leahy, "House Rules," *Washington Post Magazine*, June 3, 2007.

19. Joe Courtney for Congress Web site: www.joecourtney.com.

20. Dotty LeMieux, "Ten Common Mistakes Novice Candidates Make."

21. Max Cleland, "'Wire-Side' Chat with Senator Max Cleland," *Trail Mix*, April 30, 2006.

22. Ibid.

23. Max Cleland, press release, August 1, 2006.

CHAPTER 5

1. Brad Martin, "Beer Ice Ammo interview," *Trail Mix*, September 22, 2006.

2. Brad Martin, speech (May 26, 2007).

3. Ibid.

4. Andrea Dew Steele, interview, May 2007.

5. Lezlee Westine, interview, June 12, 2007.

6. Will Durst, interview, April 10, 2007.

7. Markos Moulitsas, e-mail, June 25, 2007.

8. Rahm Emanuel, conference call, April 17, 2006.

9. Kathy Kiely, "'New Direction' Is New Theme for Democratic Plan," *USA Today*, June 13, 2006.

10. Edward Epstein, "GOP Polishes Up Agenda Catering to Conservative Base," *San Francisco Chronicle*, July 7, 2006, http:// www.sfgate.com/cgi-bin/article.cgi?file=/chronicle/archive/2006/ 07/07/MNG7JJRCE41.DTL&type=politics.

11. George Ray, speech (San Francisco, May 26, 2007).

12. Bill Press, e-mail, July 19, 2007.

13. John Halpin, James Heidbreder, Mark Lloyd, Paul Woodhull, Ben Scott, Josh Silver, and S. Derek Turner, *The Structural Imbalance of Political Talk Radio* (Washington, D.C.: The Center for American Progress and Free Press, 2007).

14. Bill Press, e-mail, July 19, 2007.

15. Lezlee Westine, e-mail, June 12, 2007.

16. Markos Moulitsas, e-mail, June 25, 2007.

17. Lee Rainie, and John Horrigan, "Election 2006 Online," The Pew Research Center, www.pewinternet.org/pdfs/PIP _Politics_2006.pdf.

18. "2006 Political Blogs Reader Survey," Blogads, www.blogads.com/survey/blog_reader_surveys_overview.html.

19. Cyrus Krohn, speech (May 26, 2007).

20. Arianna Huffington, "Be a Part of HuffPost's Online-Only

Presidential Candidate Mashup," *Huffington Post*, August 2, 2007, http://www.huffingtonpost.com/arianna-huffington/be-a-part-of-huffposts-o_b_58859.html?view=screen.

21. Jack Brady, speech (May 25, 2007).

22. Phil Matier and Andy Ross, interview, March 22, 2007.

23. Ibid.

24. Brad Martin, interview, July 2007.

25. Matier and Ross, interview, March 22, 2007.

26. "Clinton Debate Moment," YouTube, www.youtube.com/watch?v=ta_SFvgbrlY.

27. George Lakoff, interview, June 12, 2007.

28. Bill Press, e-mail, July 19, 2007.

29. David Brock, e-mail, June 7, 2007; the Media Matters Web site is www.mediamatters.org.

30. Ibid.

31. Kerry Kennedy, interview, April 4, 2007.

32. Fred Ross Sr., "Axioms for Organizers."

CHAPTER 6

1. LeMieux, "Ten Common Mistakes Novice Candidates Make."

2. Ibid.

3. Rachel Binah, e-mail, May 16, 2007.

4. Ibid.

5. Brian Wolff, e-mail, May 20, 2007.

6. Ibid.

7. Brian Wolff, interview, June 21, 2007.

8. Chris Murphy, discussion, June 6, 2007; Chris Murphy for Congress Web site: www.murphyforcongress.org.

9. Tim Tagaris, e-mail, June 2, 2007.

CHAPTER 7

1. Chris Finnie, e-mail, July 14, 2007.

2. James Zogby, e-mail, May 2007.

3. DemocracyAction Web site: www.democracyaction.org.

4. Thom O'Shaughnessy, e-mail, May 31, 2007.

5. Excerpted from Fred Ross Jr., foreword to *Cesar Chavez*.

6. Ed Perlmutter for Congress Web site: www.perlmutterfor colorado.com.

7. Donnie Fowler, interview, March 7, 2007.

8. Sam Gedjenson, interview, May 19, 2007; Hilltop Brigade Web site: www.hilltopbrigade.org.

9. Thom O'Shaughnessy, e-mail, May 31, 2007.

10. Reagan Reagan, "Remarks in New York City at a Reception for Delegates to the State Republican Convention (June 17, 1982), http://www.reagan.utexas.edu/archives/speeches/1982/61782e.htm.

11. Brad Martin, "Best Practices for Primary Winners," *Trail Mix*, June 15, 2006.

12. Ron Klein, discussion, April 7, 2006; Peter Wallsten and Tom Hamburger, "Two Parties Far Apart in Turnout Tactics Too," *Los Angeles Times*, November 6, 2006.

13. *USA Today*, November 1, 2006, www.usatoday.com/news/washington/2006-11-01-bush-camaign_x.htm.

14. Bill Clinton, speech, liveblogged by the author from John Lewis' front porch, Atlanta, GA, October 25, 2006.

15. Al Gore, speech (Cabrini College, Radnor Township, PA, November 3, 2006).

16. Bush campaign 2000 coverage from *Journeys with George*, directed by Alexandra Pelosi (HBO, 2003); transcript with permission of Alexandra Pelosi.

17. Donnie Fowler, interview, June 13, 2007.

18. *Meet the Press*, NBC, November 4, 2006.

19. Donna Brazile, e-mail, June 4, 2007.

20. Howard Dean, quoted on Democratic National Committee's Web site, www.democrats.org, November 6, 2006.

Index

About the Author

Author, attorney, and activist Christine Pelosi has engaged in extensive voter contact, education, and mobilization efforts at the local, state, and federal levels. She has served as executive director of the California Democratic Party, deputy city attorney and assistant district attorney for the City of San Francisco, special counsel in the U.S. Department of Housing and Urban Development, and chief of staff to U.S. Congressman John F. Tierney. Since 1996, she has chaired the California Democratic Party Platform Committee and served as an elected member of the Democratic National Committee, where she cofounded the DNC Veterans and Military Families Council. *Campaign Boot Camp: Basic Training for Future Leaders* emerged from her years of grassroots activism and her service as director of the AFSCME PEOPLE/New House PAC Congressional Candidates Boot Camp, which worked with over forty challengers in 2006, twelve of whom were elected to Congress. She holds a JD from the University of California Hastings College of the Law and a BSFS from Georgetown University's School of Foreign Service. An avid baseball fan, she lives within walking distance of her beloved San Francisco Giants.

Other Books from PoliPointPress

THE BLUE PAGES, *A Directory of Companies Rated by Their Politics and Practices*

Helps consumers match their buying decisions with their political values by listing the political contributions and business practices of over 1,000 companies. $9.95, PAPERBACK

JEFF COHEN, *Cable News Confidential: My Misadventures in Corporate Media*

Offers a fast-paced romp through the three major cable news channels—Fox CNN, and MSNBC—and delivers a serious message about their failure to cover the most urgent issues of the day. $14.95, PAPERBACK

MARJORIE COHN, *Cowboy Republic: Six Ways the Bush Gang Has Defied the Law*

Shows how the executive branch under President Bush has systematically defied the law instead of enforcing it. $14.95, PAPERBACK

JOE CONASON, *The Raw Deal: How the Bush Republicans Plan to Destroy Social Security and the Legacy of the New Deal*

Reveals the well-financed and determined effort to undo the Social Security Act and other New Deal programs. $11.00, PAPERBACK

KEVIN DANAHER, SHANNON BIGGS, *and* JASON MARK, *Building the Green Economy: Success Stories from the Grassroots*

Shows how community groups, families, and individual citizens have protected their food and water, cleaned up their neighborhoods, and strengthened their local economies. $16.00, PAPERBACK

REESE ERLICH, *The Iran Agenda: The Real Story of U.S. Policy and the Middle East Crisis*

Explores the turbulent recent history between the two countries and how it has led to a showdown over nuclear technology. $14.95, PAPERBACK

STEVEN HILL, *10 Steps to Repair American Democracy*

Identifies the key problems with American democracy, especially election practices, and proposes ten specific reforms to reinvigorate it. $11.00, PAPERBACK

YVONNE LATTY, *In Conflict: Iraq War Veterans Speak Out on Duty, Loss, and the Fight to Stay Alive*
Features the unheard voices, extraordinary experiences, and personal photographs of a broad mix of Iraq War veterans, including Congressman Patrick Murphy, Tammy Duckworth, Kelly Daugherty, and Camilo Mejia. $24.00, HARDCOVER

PHILLIP LONGMAN, *Best Care Anywhere: Why VA Health Care Is Better Than Yours*
Shows how the turnaround at the long-maligned VA hospitals provides a blueprint for salvaging America's expensive but troubled health care system. $14.95, PAPERBACK

WILLIAM RIVERS PITT, *House of Ill Repute: Reflections on War, Lies, and America's Ravaged Reputation*
Skewers the Bush Administration for its reckless invasions, warrantless wiretaps, lethally incompetent response to Hurricane Katrina, and other scandals and blunders. $16.00, PAPERBACK

NOMI PRINS, *Jacked:* How *"Conservatives" Are Picking Your Pocket—Whether You Voted For Them or Not*
Describes how the "conservative" agenda has affected your wallet, skewed national priorities, and diminished America—but not the American spirit. $12.00, PAPERBACK

NORMAN SOLOMON, *Made Love, Got War: Close Encounters with America's Warfare State*
Traces five decades of American militarism and the media's all-too-frequent failure to challenge it. $24.95, HARDCOVER

JOHN SPERLING *et al.*, *The Great Divide: Retro vs. Metro America*
Explains how and why our nation is so bitterly divided into what the authors call Retro and Metro America. $19.95, PAPERBACK

CURTIS WHITE, *The Spirit of Disobedience: Resisting the Charms of Fake Politics, Mindless Consumption, and the Culture of Total Work*
Debunks the notion that liberalism has no need for spirituality and describes a "middle way" through our red state/blue state political impasse. Includes three powerful interviews with John DeGraaf, James Howard Kunstler, and Michael Ableman. $24.00, HARDCOVER

For more information, please visit www.p3books.com.

About This Book

This book is printed on Cascade Enviro100 Print paper. It contains 100 percent post-consumer fiber and is certified EcoLogo, Processed Chlorine Free, and FSC Recycled. For each ton used instead of virgin paper, we:

- Save the equivalent of 17 trees
- Reduce air emissions by 2,098 pounds
- Reduce solid waste by 1,081 pounds
- Reduce the water used by 10,196 gallons
- Reduce suspended particles in the water by 6.9 pounds.

This paper is manufactured using biogas energy, reducing natural gas consumption by 2,748 cubic feet per ton of paper produced.

The book's printer, Malloy Incorporated, works with paper mills that are environmentally responsible, that do not source fiber from endangered forests, and that are third-party certified. Malloy prints with soy and vegetable based inks, and over 98 percent of the solid material they discard is recycled. Their water emissions are entirely safe for disposal into their municipal sanitary sewer system, and they work with the Michigan Department of Environmental Quality to ensure that their air emissions meet all environmental standards.

The Michigan Department of Environmental Quality has recognized Malloy as a Great Printer for their compliance with environmental regulations, written environmental policy, pollution prevention efforts, and pledge to share best practices with other printers. Their county Department of Planning and Environment has designated them a Waste Knot Partner for their waste prevention and recycling programs.